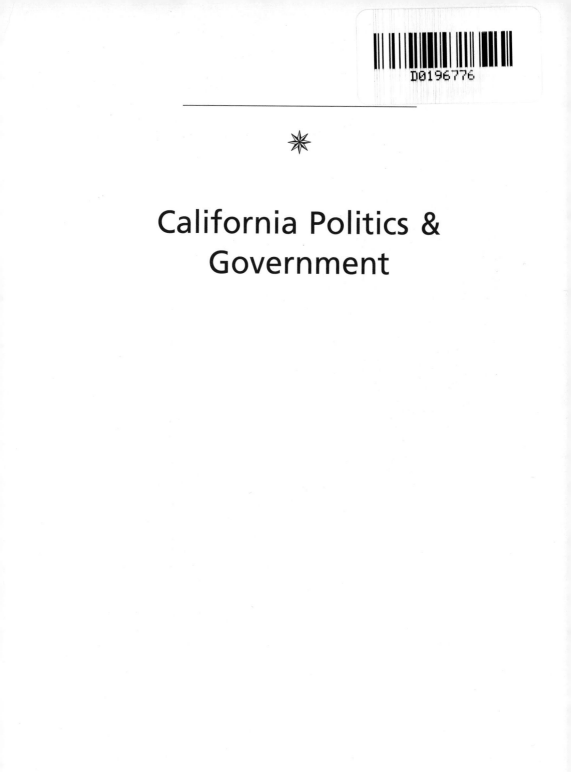

✳

California Politics & Government

California Politics & Government

A Practical Approach

TWELFTH EDITION

LARRY N. GERSTON
San Jose State University

TERRY CHRISTENSEN
San Jose State University

WADSWORTH
CENGAGE Learning·

Australia · Brazil · Japan · Korea · Mexico · Singapore · Spain · United Kingdom · United States

WADSWORTH
CENGAGE Learning·

California Politics & Government: A Practical Approach, Twelfth Edition

Larry N. Gerston and Terry Christensen

Senior Publisher: Suzanne Jeans

Executive Editor: Carolyn Merrill

Assistant Editor: Patrick Roach

Editorial Assistant: Eireann Aspell

Media Editor: Laura Hildebrand

Brand Manager: Lydia LeStar

Marketing Communications Manager: Kyle Zimmerman

Rights Acquisitions Specialist: Jennifer Meyer Dare

Manufacturing Planner: Fola Orkoya

Art and Design Direction, Production Management, and Composition: PreMediaGlobal

Cover Image: © Bobkeenan Photography/Shutterstock & © Maxym Boner/iStockphoto

For product information and technology assistance, contact us at **Cengage Learning Customer & Sales Support, 1-800-354-9706**

For permission to use material from this text or product, submit all requests online at **www.cengage.com/permissions**
Further permissions questions can be emailed to
permissionrequest@cengage.com

Library of Congress Control Number: 2012954710

ISBN-13: 978-1-133-58765-1

ISBN-10: 1-133-58765-8

Wadsworth
20 Channel Center Street
Boston, MA 02210
USA

Cengage Learning is a leading provider of customized learning solutions with office locations around the globe, including Singapore, the United Kingdom, Australia, Mexico, Brazil and Japan. Locate your local office at **international.cengage.com/region**

Cengage Learning products are represented in Canada by Nelson Education, Ltd.

For your course and learning solutions, visit
www.cengage.com

Purchase any of our products at your local college store or at our preferred online store **www.cengagebrain.com**

Instructors: Please visit **login.cengage.com** and log in to access instructor-specific resources.

Printed in the United States of America
2 3 4 5 6 7 16 15 14 13

✳

To the futures of Adam and Jodi, Lee, and Rachel Gerston
and the memories of Anna and Teter Christensen and Tillie and Chester Welliever

Contents

Preface

Ask someone to describe California and it's amazing what answers you will hear. Some view California as a land of endless opportunity; others cast the state as the political equivalent of one huge congested freeway mired in hopeless gridlock. Both characterizations have merit along with so many others.

California reminds us of a powerful, rich symphony adorned with a full complement of instruments played by the most talented artists. Yet, when the conductor brings down his baton, the brilliant sounds don't quite mesh. And while it is a state with seemingly limitless horizons for some, it can discourage so many others just trying to get by. Few states possess as many conflicting forces as California. Given its multifaceted composition, we marvel that anything ever moves anywhere but sideways.

Yet its complexity is what makes California so deceptively alluring, if frustrating. Just when you think you have it figured out, you realize that there's yet another layer to examine along with the rest, another facet that marginalizes any conclusions reached to that point. California is a political conundrum, to say the least, which is why we are so fascinated with the state, its people, and its politics.

This edition, our twelfth, proceeds two years after the previous edition, identical to the interims between all of our other editions. Some have asked us why we keep to such a tight writing schedule. You know the answer if you watch California—too many things happen too fast. For that reason, this edition is no different in chronicling the immense changes that have occurred over the past two years.

Since our last post, California has once again revealed its fickleness. On the one hand, we have witnessed new directions. The impact of the 2012 election, brand new legislative and congressional districts courtesy of the Citizens Independent Redistricting Commission, the "top two" primary system, bankrupt local governments, social media breakthroughs, and new state/federal arrangements are among the many changes that have appeared in this short period of time, all of which are discussed along with many others in this volume.

On the other hand, California remains just as plagued by lingering problems today as in the past. It continues to be a state with a terrible imbalance between revenue and spending, a stubbornly weak economy, a society that reveals a huge chasm between those who have and those who don't, an infrastructure in tatters, the growing tension among various racial and ethnic groups, and a political system as disjointed today as any time in the past. These all bear additional discussion because of their seeming permanence, if for no other reason.

There is so much to write about this once-Golden State yet, as with our previous editions, we remain committed to fulfilling our mandate with brevity and as much clarity as possible. We don't linger on themes as much as we try to introduce and connect them in the "nuts and bolts" fashion that has guided our previous efforts. For those who want to know more, we offer additional source materials at the end of each chapter through books and various websites.

Meanwhile, as you explore this book, we hope that you will share our excitement about a state unequalled by any other. Whatever California's future, it surely will be influenced by its rich past and present.

Many have assisted us in our effort to provide the best assessment possible on California. Our friends in politics, the media, and elected office, as well as fellow academics, have provided valuable counsel, information, and insights at various junctures. We would especially like to thank the following reviewers whose comments helped mold this edition: Stephanie Burkhalter, Humboldt State; Traci Fahimi, Irvine Valley College; and John Roche, Palomar College. Most of all, we continue to benefit from our students who, with their penetrating questions and thoughtful observations, push us to explore and report on topics that we might not have considered otherwise. Some have gone on to political careers in local, state, and federal offices, helping us to believe that the next generation is prepared and willing to take ownership of the state and its potential.

Finally, we are indebted to the attentive production staff at Cengage, who artfully managed an incredibly tight schedule to facilitate production within weeks of the November 6, 2012, election. They include Carolyn Merrill, Executive Political Science Editor; Anita Devine, Political Science Acquisitions Editor; Patrick Roach; Assistant Political Science Editor; and Lydia LeStar, Brand Manager, who patiently and efficiently worked with us from manuscript to page proofs. All these people and many others assisted this project to the best of our abilities. Of course, in the end responsibility for the product is ours.

About the Authors

Larry N. Gerston, Professor Emeritus of Political Science at San Jose State University, interacts with the political process as both an author and an observer. As an author, he has written ten academic books in addition to *California Politics and Government: A Practical Approach*, including *Making Public Policy: From Conflict to Resolution (1983)*, *Politics in the Golden State* (with Terry Christensen, 1984), *The Deregulated Society* (with Cynthia Fraleigh and Robert Schwab, 1988), *American Government: Politics, Process, and Policies* (1993), *Public Policy: Process and Principles* (1987), *Public Policymaking in a Democratic Society: A Guide to Civic Engagement* (2002), *Recall! California's Political Earthquake* (with Christensen, 2004), *American Federalism: A Concise Introduction* (2007), *Confronting Reality: Ten Issues Threatening to Implode American Society and How We Can Fix It* (2009), and *Not So Golden After All: The Rise and Fall of California* (2012). As an observer, Gerston serves as the political analyst for NBC11, a San Francisco Bay Area television station, where he appears on a regular basis. He has written more than a hundred op-ed pieces for newspapers throughout the nation and speaks often on issues such as civic engagement and personal political empowerment.

Terry Christensen is a San Jose State University Professor Emeritus of Political Science. Among his other awards for scholarship and service to the university, he was named Outstanding Professor in 1998. He is the author or co-author of nine books and frequent newspaper op-ed pieces. Local and national media regularly call on him for analysis of politics in California and Silicon Valley. In addition to other books co-authored with Larry Gerston, his works include *Projecting Politics: Political Messages in American Films* (2005), co-authored by Peter Haas, and *Local Politics: A Practical Guide to Governing at the Grassroots* (2006), co-authored by Tom Hogen-Esch. Christensen is experienced in practical politics at the local level as an advocate of policy proposals, an adviser to grassroots groups, and an adviser and mentor to candidates for local office—many of whom are his former students. He has served on numerous civic committees and commissions. He was the founding executive director of CommUniverCity San Jose (www.communivercitysanjose.org), a partnership between the City of San Jose, San Jose State University, and adjacent neighborhoods. Through CommUniverCity, hundreds of students are learning about life and politics in their community through service projects selected by neighborhood residents and supported by the city.

SUPPLEMENTS FOR INSTRUCTORS

Instructor's Manual with Test Bank Online for Gerston/Christensen *California Politics and Government: A Practical Approach*, **12e**

- IBSN-13: 9781133591382

- This password-protected Instructor's Manual and Test Bank are accessible by logging into your account at www.cengage.com/login.

1

California's People, Economy, and Politics: Yesterday, Today, and Tomorrow

CHAPTER CONTENTS

Thanks to the Gold Rush, the Golden Gate Bridge, and over a century of booming growth, California has long been known as "the Golden State," but today some say the Golden State no longer glitters. Googling "California as a failed state" (like Somalia or Greece) produces over 70 million hits. California's economy has been mired in recession since 2007 and the state has suffered over a decade of budget deficits while politics in the state capital seems stuck in gridlock. To many, California politics seems turbulent and unpredictable. Political leaders rise and fall precipitately. Wealthy candidates and special interests are accused of "buying" elections. While state government stalls in gridlock, issues are referred to the voters, who are often confused by complex and sometimes obscure ballot measures. Some say this is democracy gone mad; others have concluded that California is ungovernable.

But however volatile or dysfunctional California politics may seem, it is serious business that affects us all, and it can be understood by examining the history and present characteristics of our state—especially its changing population and economy. Wave after wave of immigrants have made California a diverse, multicultural society, while new technologies repeatedly transform the state's economy. The resulting disparate demographic and economic interests compete for the benefits and protections conferred by government and thus shape the state's politics. To understand California today—and tomorrow—we need to know a little about its past and about the development of the competing interests within the state.

COLONIZATION, REBELLION, AND STATEHOOD

The first Californians probably were immigrants like the rest of us. Archaeologists believe that the ancestors of American Indians crossed an ice or land bridge or traveled by sea from Asia to Alaska thousands of years ago and then headed south. Europeans began exploring the California coast in the early 1500s, but colonization didn't start until 1769, when the Spanish established a string of missions and military outposts. About 300,000 Native Americans were living here then, mostly near the coast.

These native Californians were brought to the missions as Catholic converts and workers, but European diseases and the destruction of the native culture reduced their numbers to about 100,000 by 1849. Entire tribes were wiped out and the Indian population continued to diminish throughout the nineteenth century. Today, less than 1 percent of California's population is Native American, and many feel alienated from a society that has overwhelmed their peoples, cultures, and traditions. Chronic poverty, however, has been alleviated for some by the development of casinos on native lands, a phenomenon that has also made some tribes major players in state politics.

Apart from building missions, the Spaniards did little to develop their faraway possession. Not much changed when Mexico (including California) declared its independence from Spain in 1822. A few thousand Mexicans quietly raised cattle on vast ranches and built small towns around their central plazas.

Meanwhile, advocates of expansion in the United States coveted California's rich lands and access to the Pacific Ocean. When Mexico and the United States went to war over Texas in 1846, Yankee immigrants to California seized the moment and declared independence from Mexico. After the U.S. victory, Mexico surrendered its claim to lands extending from Texas to California. By this time, foreigners already outnumbered Californians of Spanish ancestry 9,000 to 7,500.

Gold was discovered in 1848, and the '49ers who started arriving in hordes the next year brought the nonnative population to 264,000 by 1852. Many immigrants came directly from Europe. The first Chinese people also arrived to work in the mines, which yielded more than a billion dollars' worth of gold in five years.

The surge in population and commerce moved the new Californians to political action. A constitutional convention consisting of forty-eight delegates (only seven of whom were native Californians) assembled the Constitution of 1849 by cutting and pasting from the constitutions of existing states; the convention requested statehood, which the U.S. Congress quickly granted. The constitutional structure of the new state approximated what we have today, with a two-house legislature; a supreme court; and an executive branch consisting of a governor, lieutenant governor, controller, attorney general, and superintendent of public instruction. The constitution also included a bill of rights, but only white males were allowed to vote. California's Chinese, African American, and Native American residents were soon prohibited by law from owning land, testifying in court, or attending public schools.

The voters approved the constitution, and San Jose became the first state capital. With housing in short supply, many newly elected legislators had to lodge in tents, and the primitive living conditions were exacerbated by heavy rain and flooding. The state capital soon moved on to Vallejo and Benicia, finally settling in 1854 in Sacramento—closer to the gold fields.

As the Gold Rush ended, a land rush began. Small homesteads were common in other states because of federal ownership and allocation of land, but California had been divided into huge tracts by Spanish and Mexican land grants. As early as 1870, a few hundred men owned most of the farmland. Their ranches were the forerunners of the agribusiness corporations of today, and as the mainstay of the state's economy, they exercised even more clout than their modern successors.

In less than fifty years, California had belonged to three different nations. During the same period, its economy and population had changed dramatically as hundreds of thousands of immigrants from all over the world came to claim their share of the "Golden State." The pattern of a rapidly evolving, multicultural polity was set.

RAILROADS, MACHINES, AND REFORM

Technology wrought the next transformation in the form of railroads. In 1861 Sacramento merchants led by Leland Stanford founded the railroad that would become the **Southern Pacific Railroad**. They persuaded Congress to provide millions of dollars in land grants and loan subsidies for a railroad linking California with the eastern United States, thus greatly expanding the market for California's products. Stanford became governor and used his influence to provide state assistance. Cities and counties also contributed—under the threat of being bypassed by the railroad. To obtain workers at cheap rates, the railroad builders imported 15,000 Chinese laborers.

When the transcontinental track was completed in 1869, the Southern Pacific expanded its system throughout the state by building new lines and buying up existing ones. The railroad crushed competitors by cutting shipping charges, and by the 1880s it had become the state's dominant transportation company, as well as its largest private landowner with 11 percent of the entire state. With its business agents doubling as political representatives in almost every

California city and county, the Southern Pacific soon developed a formidable political machine. "The Octopus," as novelist Frank Norris called the railroad, placed allies in state and local offices through its control of both the Republican and Democratic parties. Once there, these officials protected the interests of the Southern Pacific if they wanted to continue in office. County tax assessors who were supported by the political machine set favorable tax rates for the railroad and its allies, while the machine-controlled legislature ensured a hands-off policy by state government.

THE WORKINGMEN'S PARTY

People in small towns and rural areas who were unwilling to support the machine lost jobs, businesses, and other benefits. Some moved to cities, especially San Francisco, where manufacturing jobs were available. Chinese workers who had been brought to California to build the railroad also sought work in the cities when it was completed. But when a depression in the 1870s made jobs scarce, these newcomers faced hostile treatment from earlier immigrants. Led by Denis Kearney, Irish immigrants became the core of the **Workingmen's Party**, a political organization that blamed economic difficulties on the railroad and the Chinese.

Small farmers who opposed the railroad united through the Grange movement. In 1879 the Grangers and the Workingmen's Party called California's second constitutional convention in hopes of breaking the railroad's hold on the state. The **Constitution of 1879** mandated regulation of railroads, utilities, banks, and corporations. An elected State Board of Equalization was set up to ensure the fairness of local tax assessments on railroads and their friends, as well as their enemies. The new constitution also prohibited the Chinese from owning land, voting, or working for state or local government.

The railroad soon reclaimed power, however, by taking control of the agencies that were created to regulate it. Nonetheless, efforts to regulate big business and control racial relations became recurring themes in California life and politics, and much of the Constitution of 1879 remains intact today.

THE PROGRESSIVES

The growth fostered by the railroad eventually produced a new middle class of merchants, doctors, lawyers, teachers, and skilled workers who were not dependent on the railroad. They objected to the corrupt practices and favoritism of the railroad's political machine, which they thought was restraining economic development in their communities. This new middle class demanded honesty and competence, which they called "good government." In 1907 some of these crusaders established the Lincoln-Roosevelt League, a reform group within the Republican Party, and became part of the national Progressive movement. Their leader, Hiram Johnson, was elected governor in 1910; they also captured control of the state legislature.

To break the power of the machine, the **Progressives** introduced a wave of reforms that shape California politics to this day. Predictably, they created a new regulatory agency for the railroads and utilities, the Public Utilities Commission (PUC). Most of their reforms, however, aimed at weakening the political parties as tools of bosses and machines. Instead of party bosses handpicking candidates at party conventions, the voters now were given the power to select their party's nominees for office in primary elections. Cross-filing further diluted party power by allowing candidates to file for and win the nominations of more than one political party. The Progressives made city and county elections "nonpartisan" by removing party labels from local ballots altogether. They also created a civil service system to select state employees on the basis of their qualifications rather than their political connections.

Finally, the Progressives introduced direct democracy, which allowed the voters to amend the constitution and create laws through initiatives, repeal laws through referenda and to recall, or remove, elected officials before their terms expired. Supporters of an initiative, referendum, or recall must circulate petitions and collect a specified number of signatures of registered voters before it goes to the voters.

Like the Workingmen's Party before them, the Progressives were concerned about immigration. Antagonism toward recent Japanese immigrants (who numbered 72,000 by 1910) resulted in Progressive support for a ban on land ownership by aliens and the National Immigration Act of 1924, which effectively halted Asian immigration. Other, more positive changes by the Progressives included giving women the right to vote, passing child labor and workers' compensation laws, and implementing conservation programs to protect natural resources.

Thanks to the Progressive reforms, the railroad's political machine eventually died, although California's increasingly diverse economy also weakened the machine, as the emerging oil, automobile, and trucking industries gave the state alternative means of transportation and shipping. These and other growing industries ultimately restructured economic and political power in California.

The reform movement waned in the 1920s, but the Progressive legacy of weak political parties and direct democracy opened up California's politics to its citizens, as well as to powerful interest groups and individual candidates with strong personalities. A long and detailed constitution is also part of the legacy. The Progressives instituted their reforms by amending (and thus lengthening) the Constitution of 1879 rather than calling for a new constitutional convention. Direct democracy subsequently enabled voters and interest groups to amend the constitution, constantly adding to its length.

THE GREAT DEPRESSION AND WORLD WAR II

California's population grew by more than 2 million in the 1920s (see Table 1.1). Many newcomers headed for Los Angeles, where employment opportunities in shipping, filmmaking, and manufacturing (of clothing, automobiles, and aircraft) abounded. Then came the Great Depression of the 1930s, which saw the unemployment rate soar from 3 percent in 1925 to 33 percent by 1933. Even so, more

TABLE 1.1 California's Population Growth, 1850–2010

Year	Population	Percentage of U.S. Population
1850	93,000	0.4
1900	1,485,000	2.0
1950	10,643,000	7.0
1970	20,039,000	9.8
1990	29,733,000	11.7
2010	37,253,956	12.0

SOURCE: U.S. Census.

than a million people came to California, including thousands of poor white immigrants from the "dust bowl" of the drought-impacted Midwest. Many wandered through California's great Central Valley in search of work, displacing Mexicans—who earlier had supplanted the Chinese and Japanese—as farm workers. Racial antagonism ran high, and many Mexicans were arbitrarily sent back to Mexico. Labor unrest reached a crescendo in the early 1930s, as workers on farms, in canneries, and on the docks of San Francisco and Los Angeles fought for higher wages and an eight-hour workday.

The immigrants and union activists of the 1920s and 1930s also changed California politics. Many registered as Democrats, thus challenging the dominant Republicans. The Depression and President Franklin Roosevelt's popular New Deal helped the Democrats become California's majority party in registration, although winning elections proved more difficult. The Democrats finally gained the governorship in 1938, but their candidate, Culbert Olson, was the only Democratic winner between 1894 and 1958.

World War II revived the economic boom, but even in the 1930s, the state and federal governments were investing in California's future, building the Golden Gate Bridge and the Central Valley Project whose dams and canals brought water to the desert and reaffirmed agriculture as a mainstay of California's economy. Then between 1940 and 1946, the federal government spent $35 billion in California, creating 500,000 defense industry jobs. California's radio, electronics, and aircraft industries grew at phenomenal rates. The jobs brought new immigrants, including many African Americans, whose proportion of the state's population quadrupled during the 1940s.

Meanwhile, California's Japanese and Mexican American residents became victims of racial conflict. During the war, 120,000 Japanese Americans, suspected of loyalty to their ancestral homeland, were sent to prison camps (officially called internment centers). Antagonism toward Mexican Americans resulted in the Zoot Suit Riots in Los Angeles in 1943, when Anglo sailors and police attacked Mexican Americans wearing distinctive suits featuring long jackets with wide lapels, padded shoulders, and high-waisted, pegged pants.

Although the voters chose a Democratic governor during the Great Depression, they returned to the Republican fold as the economy revived. Earl Warren, one of a new breed of moderate Republicans, was elected governor in 1942, 1946, and 1950, becoming the only individual to win the office three times until Jerry Brown was elected in 2010. Warren used cross-filing to win the nominations of both parties and staked out a relationship with the voters that he claimed was above party politics. A classic example of California's personality-oriented politics, Warren left the state in 1953 to become chief justice of the U.S. Supreme Court.

GROWTH, CHANGE, AND POLITICAL TURMOIL

With the Republican Party in disarray due to infighting, Californians elected a Democratic governor, Edmund G. "Pat" Brown, and a Democratic majority in the state legislature in 1958. To prevent Republicans like Warren from taking advantage of cross-filing again, the state's new leaders immediately outlawed that electoral device.

In control of both the governor's office and the legislature for the first time in the twentieth century, Democrats moved aggressively to develop the state's infrastructure. Completion of the massive California Water Project, construction of the state highway network, and creation of an unparalleled higher education system helped accommodate the growing population and stimulated the economy. Meanwhile, in the 1960s, California's black and Latino minorities became more assertive, pushing for civil rights, desegregation of schools, access to higher education, and improved treatment for California's predominantly Latino farm workers.

The demands of minority groups alienated some white voters, however, and the Democratic programs were expensive. After opening their purse strings during the eight-year tenure of Pat Brown, Californians became more cautious about the state's direction. Race riots precipitated by police brutality in Los Angeles, along with student unrest over the Vietnam War, also turned the voters against liberal Democrats such as Brown.

In 1966 Republican Ronald Reagan was elected governor; he moved the state in a more conservative direction before going on to serve as president. His successor as governor, Democrat Edmund G. "Jerry" Brown, Jr., was the son of the earlier governor Brown and a liberal on social issues. Like Reagan, however, the younger Brown led California away from spending on growth-inducing infrastructure, such as highways and schools. In 1978 the voters solidified this change with the watershed tax-cutting initiative, Proposition 13 (see Chapter 8). Although Democrats still outnumbered Republicans among California's registered voters, two Republicans succeeded Brown as governor.

In 1998 California elected Gray Davis, its first Democratic governor in sixteen years. He was reelected in 2002 despite voter concerns about an energy crisis, a recession, and a growing budget deficit. As a consequence of these crises and what some perceived as an arrogant attitude, Davis faced an unprecedented recall election in October 2003. The voters removed him from office and replaced him with Republican Arnold Schwarzenegger. Then in 2010, former governor Jerry Brown was elected governor in a dramatic comeback, making history as California's youngest and oldest governor.

Democrats have had more consistent success in the state legislature and the congressional delegation, where they have dominated since 1960. California voters have also opted for Democrats in every presidential election since 1988.

But recurring conflicts between a Democratic legislature and Republican chief executives have made governing California challenging, a situation that, until 2010, was exacerbated by the constitutional requirement for a supermajority to enact the state budget. Meanwhile, the voters have become increasingly involved in policymaking by initiative and referendum (see Chapter 2). Amendments to California's constitution, which require voter approval, appear on almost every state ballot. As a consequence, California's Constitution of 1879 has been amended over five hundred times; the U.S. Constitution includes just twenty-seven amendments.

Throughout these changes the state's population continued to grow, outpacing most other states so much that the California delegation to the U.S. House of Representatives now numbers fifty-three—more than twenty-one other states combined. Much of this growth was the result of a new wave of immigration facilitated by more flexible national immigration laws during the 1960s and 1970s. Immigration from Asia—especially from Southeast Asia after the Vietnam War—increased greatly. A national amnesty for undocumented residents also enabled many Mexicans to gain citizenship and bring their families from Mexico. In all, 85 percent of the 6 million newcomers and births in California in the 1980s were Asian, Latino, or black. Growth slowed in the 1990s, as 2 million more people left the state than came to it from other states, but California's population continued to increase as a result of births and immigration from abroad. In 1990 whites made up 57 percent of the state's population; by 2010 they were 40 percent.

Constantly increasing diversity enlivened California's culture and provided a steady flow of new workers, but it also increased tensions. Some affluent Californians retreated to gated communities; others fled the state. Racial conflict broke out between gangs on the streets and in prisons. As in difficult economic times throughout California's history, a recession during the early 1990s led many Californians to blame immigrants, especially those who were in California illegally. A series of ballot measures raised divisive race-related issues such as illegal immigration, bilingualism, and affirmative action. The issue of immigration enflames California politics to this day, although the increasing electoral clout of minorities has provided some balance.

CALIFORNIA TODAY

If California were an independent nation, its economy would rank ninth in the world, with an annual gross national product of nearly $2 trillion. Much of the state's strength stems from its economic diversity (see Table 1.2). The elements of this diversity also constitute powerful political interests in state politics.

Half of California—mostly desert and mountains—is owned by the state and federal governments. In rural areas, a few big corporations control much of the state's rich farmlands. These enormous agribusinesses make California the

TABLE 1.2 California's Economy

Industrial Sector	Employees	Amount (in millions)
Professional and business services	2,218,900	$ 272,248
Education and health services	1,881,300	149,884
Leisure and hospitality services	1,575,800	81,094
Other services	484,000	47,617
Information	451,700	136,046
Government	2,378,300	224,720
Trade, transportation, and utilities	2,715,200	300,789
Manufacturing	1,242,700	229,862
Finance, insurance, and real estate	775,100	405,260
Construction	574,500	58,959
Mining and natural resources	29,200	52,425
Agriculture	376,700	37,500
Total, all sectors	14,703,400	$1,996,404

SOURCE: California Employment Development Department, www.labormarketinfo.edd.ca.gov (accessed July 2012); and U.S. Department of Commerce, Bureau of Economic Analysis, *Survey of Current Business*, June 2012, http://www.bea.gov /scb/pdf/2012 (accessed July 2012).

nation's leading farm state, producing more than four hundred different food-stuffs, including nearly half of the vegetables, fruits, and nuts and 21 percent of the dairy products consumed nationally. Grapes and wine are also top products, with thousands of growers and 3,364 wineries.

State politics affects this huge economic force in many ways, but most notably in labor relations, environmental regulation, and water supply. Farmers and their employees have battled for decades over issues ranging from wages to safety. Beginning in the 1960s, under the leadership of Cesar Chavez and the United Farm Workers union, laborers organized. Supported by public boycotts of certain farm products, they achieved some improvements in working conditions, but the struggle continues today. California's agricultural industry is also caught up in environmental issues, including the pesticide use and water pollution. In addition, booming growth in the Central Valley has urbanized some farmland, bringing "city" problems such as traffic and crowded schools to once-rural areas. The biggest issue, however, is always water. Most of California's cities and farms must import water from other parts of the state. Thanks to government subsidies, farmers claim 80 percent of the state's water supply at prices so low that they have little reason to improve inefficient irrigation systems. Meanwhile, the growth of urban areas is limited by water supplies. Today, agriculture—and water—is in the thick of California politics as the state strives to balance an essential and powerful industry with the interests of its other citizens.

Agriculture is big business, but many more Californians work in manufacturing, especially in the aerospace, defense, and high-tech industries. Employment in manufacturing, however, has declined in California in recent years, especially after the federal government reduced military and defense spending in the 1990s when the collapse of communism in the Soviet Union brought an end to the Cold War. Jobs in California shifted to postindustrial occupations such as retail sales, tourism, and services, although jobs in these sectors often pay low wages. Government policies on growth, the environment, and taxation affect all of these employment sectors, and all suffer when any one sector goes into a slump.

But the salvation of California's economy is innovation, especially in telecommunications, entertainment, medical equipment, international trade, and high-tech businesses spawned by defense and aerospace companies. In the 1990s, California hosted one-fourth of the nation's high-tech firms, which provided nearly a million jobs. Half of the nation's computer engineers worked in Silicon Valley, named after the silicon chip that revolutionized the computer industry. Running between San Jose and San Francisco, Silicon Valley became a center for innovation in technology from computers to software and Internet-based businesses, including iconic companies like Hewlett-Packard, Intel, Facebook, and Google, which are headquartered there. Biomedical and pharmaceutical companies also proliferated, further contributing to California's transformation.

Computer technology also spurred rapid expansion of the entertainment industry, long a key component of California's economy. This growth particularly benefited the Los Angeles area. Besides film and television production, tourism remains a bastion of the economy, with California regularly ranking first among the states in visitors. Along with agriculture, high-tech, telecommunications, and other industries, these businesses have made California a leader in both international and domestic trade. All these industries are part of a globalized economy, with huge amounts of trade going through the massive port complex of Los Angeles/Long Beach, as well as the San Francisco Bay Port of Oakland.

The California economy has been on a roller coaster for the past few years, though. It has been in and out of recession—first in the early 1990s, and then again after the terrible events of September 11, 2001, when the California-centered Internet boom went bust as thousands of dot-com companies failed to generate projected profits. High tech went into decline, and tens of thousands of workers lost their jobs, some of which were "off-shored" (moved to other countries). At about the same time, an energy crisis hit California; prices for gas and electricity rose and parts of the state experienced shortages of electrical power. All these factors combined to push California into a recession, with unemployment reaching 7 percent statewide and 9 percent in Silicon Valley in 2003 (the national rate was 5.9 percent). As the boom ended, tax revenues declined precipitously, producing a huge state budget deficit. Combined with the energy crisis, the deficit and other issues contributed to the recall of Governor Davis in 2003, but having a new governor didn't solve California's problems.

After a resurgence in 2006–2007, California's economy was hit by the national recession in 2009. Unemployment reached 12.4 percent in 2010 (the U.S. rate was 9.7 percent)—improving to only 10.7 percent in 2012 (U.S. = 8.2 percent). California had lost hundreds of thousands of manufacturing jobs since the 1990s as employers migrated to other states or abroad. The national home finance and foreclosure crisis also hit the California housing market and construction industry hard. Employment in all sectors, even film and television production, declined, with growth only in high tech.

Throughout its history, California has experienced economic ups and downs like these, recovered, reinvented itself, and moved on, thanks to the diversity of its economy and its people and their ability to adapt to change. While some businesses have forsaken California for other states, complaining of burdensome regulation and the high cost of doing business in California, the Public Policy Institute of California reports that the skill and higher productivity of the state's workforce, access to capital, and quality of life compensate for such costs and keep the state attractive to many businesses.[1] Innovation continues to be an economic mainstay as well. Nanotechnology companies, for example, are concentrated in the San Francisco Bay Area, while biotechnology thrives in the San Diego region and green industry (for example, solar power and electric cars) booms throughout California. Access to venture capital investment funds facilitates such innovation in California. In 2012, over half of all venture capital in the United States was invested in California; the Bay Area alone brought in $3.2 billion as compared to New York City's $588 million.[2] Another strength of the California economy is an astounding and ever-growing number of small businesses—many of which are minority-owned. Most other states lack these advantages; some are dependent on a single industry or product, and none can match the energy and optimism brought by California's constant flow of immigrants eager to take jobs in the state's new and old industries.

California's globalized economy consistently attracts more immigrants than any other state; as of 2010, 27.2 percent of the state's population was foreign born, down slightly from previous years. The foreign-born share of the U.S. population was 12.7 percent.[3] Fifty-five percent of California's immigrants are from Latin America (mostly Mexico), and 35 percent are from Asia (especially the Philippines, China, Vietnam, India, and Korea). Significantly for the California economy, 75 percent of the state's immigrant population is of working age (twenty-five to sixty-four).[4] An estimated 2 million immigrants are in California illegally.[5] As a consequence of so much immigration, 43 percent of all Californians over the age of five speak a language other than English at home,[6] resulting in a major challenge for California schools. As in past centuries, immigration and language have been hot-button political issues in California in recent years.

Table 1.3 shows the extent of California's ethnic diversity. Although non-Latino whites remain the single largest group, they are no longer a majority. Overall, the black and white proportions of California's population have

T A B L E 1.3 California's Racial and Ethnic Diversity

	1990	2000	2010
Non-Latino white	57.1%	47.3%	40.1%
Latino	26.0	32.4	37.6
Asian/Pacific Islander	9.2	11.4	13.1
Black	7.1	6.5	5.8
Native American	0.6	0.5	0.4
Mixed race	N.A.	1.9	2.6

SOURCE: U.S. Census; California Department of Finance, www.dof.ca.gov (accessed July 23, 2012). 2010 figures do not add up to 100% because 0.2% for the new classification "some other race alone" is not included in this table.

decreased, while Asian and Latino numbers have grown rapidly since the 1970s. Currently, over 70 percent of students in California's public schools are nonwhite.[7]

The realization of the California dream is not shared equally among these groups. Although the median household income as of 2010 was $60,883 according to the U.S. Census Bureau, the income of 16 percent of Californians fell below the federal poverty level—slightly above the national average, but the state's rate is considerably higher when the cost of living in California is factored in. Over half the students in California schools qualify for free or reduced-price meals.[8] The gap between rich and poor in California is among the largest in the United States and is still growing. Poverty is worst among Latinos, blacks, and Southeast Asians, who tend to hold low-paying service jobs; other Asians, along with Anglos, predominate in the more comfortable professional classes.

As the poor grow in number, some observers fear that California's middle class is vanishing. Once a majority, many of the middle class have slipped down the economic ladder, and others have simply fled the state. While many people are doing very well at the top of the ladder, more are barely getting by at the bottom, and the middle class is shrinking. The median family income in California fell by over 11 percent between 2007 and 2010; 49.7 percent of Californians were middle class as compared to 60 percent in 1980. Recent growth has concentrated in low- and high-wage jobs, and the income gap continues to widen.[9]

The costs of housing and health care are at the heart of this problem. Home prices dropped during housing crisis of 2008–2011, increasing affordability for some families, but many more suffered losses of equity in their homes, and some lost their homes to foreclosure. With a median home price of $320,540 in 2012 compared with the U.S. median of $189,400,[10] Californians still spent more of their income on housing than the national average, and fewer families were able to afford to own homes, especially in the coastal counties from San Diego to San Francisco. Homes were more affordable in inland California, however. Overall, home ownership in California lags well behind the national average, especially for Latinos and blacks. Health care is also a problem for poor and working Californians. Twenty-two percent (nearly 7 million) have no health insurance.[11]

Geographic divisions complicate California's economic and ethnic diversity. In the past, the most pronounced of these divisions was between the northern and southern portions of the state. The San Francisco Bay Area tended to be diverse, liberal, and in elections, Democratic, while Southern California was staunchly Republican and much less diverse. However, with growth and greater diversity, Los Angeles also began voting Democratic. Today, the greatest division is between the coastal and inland regions of the state (see Figure 2.3). Democrats now outnumber Republicans in San Diego, and even notoriously conservative Orange County has elected a Latina Democrat to Congress.

But even as the differences between northern and southern California fade, the contrast between coastal and inland California has increased. The state's vast Central Valley has led the way in population and job growth, with cities from Sacramento to Fresno to Bakersfield gobbling up farmland. The Inland Empire, from Riverside to San Bernardino, has grown even more rapidly since the late

1990s. Although still sparsely populated, California's northern coast, Sierra Nevada, and southern desert regions are also growing, while retaining their own distinct identities. Water, agriculture, and the environment are major issues in all these areas. Except for Sacramento, inland California is more conservative than the coastal region of the state. Perhaps ironically, the liberal counties of the coast contribute more per capita in state taxes, and the conservative inland counties receive more per capita for social service programs.[12] While coastal California remains politically dominant, the impact of inland areas on California politics increases with every election.

CALIFORNIA'S PEOPLE, ECONOMY, AND POLITICS

All these elements of California's economic, demographic, and geographic diversity vie with one another for political influence in the context of political structures that were created more than a hundred years ago. Dissatisfaction with this system has resulted in dozens of reforms by ballot measure, a recall election, and even calls for a constitutional convention to rewrite the state constitution entirely. Voter frustration is at a peak. As of 2012, only 30 percent of Californians felt that the state was "going in the right direction" (compared with 55 percent in 2007); only 39 percent approved of the governor's performance (compared with 57 percent in 2007); and 25 percent approved of the performance of the legislature (compared with 41 percent in 2007).[13] Perhaps people see California as a failed state, or maybe they're just frustrated with the current leadership. In the chapters that follow, we'll see how the diverse interests of our state operate in the current political system and gain an understanding of how it all works, why voters and others may feel frustration, and what some are doing to bring about change even as others resist.

NOTES

1. Public Policy Institute of California, "California 2025, 2012 Update," www.ppic .org (accessed July 27, 2012).

2. *San Jose Mercury News*, August 12, 2012.

3. U.S. Census, http://quickfacts.census.gov/qfd/states/06000.html (accessed July 27, 2012).

4. Hans Johnson, "Just the Facts: Immigrants in California," Public Policy Institute of California, June 2011, www.ppic.org (accessed July 27, 2012).

5. Hans Johnson, "Just the Facts: Illegal Immigrants," Public Policy Institute of California, December 2010, www.ppic.org (accessed July 27, 2012).

6. U.S. Census, op. cit.

7. "A New Diverse Majority," Southern Education Foundation, January 31, 2010, http://www.southerneducation.org/getattachment/73d87cb2-d980-4c05-a1c3-35486c2ed4b2/Publications/A-New-Diverse-Majority-Summary.aspx (accessed July 27, 2012).

8. *Ibid.*

9. Sarah Bohn and Eric Schiff, "The Great Recession and Distribution of Income in California," Public Policy Institute of California, December 2011, www.ppic.org (accessed July 27, 2012).

10. California Association of Realtors, www.car.org, and National Association of Realtors, www.realtor.org/research-and-statistics (accessed July 31, 2012).

11. California Healthcare Foundation, www.chcf.org (accessed July 31, 2012).

12. Report from the Legislative Analyst's Office cited in "California's Unequal Give and Take," *San Jose Mercury News*, June 21, 2010.

13. Public Policy Institute of California, "Statewide Survey Time Trends," www.ppic .org (accessed July 31, 2012).

LEARN MORE ON THE WEB

The California Constitution:
    www.leginfo.ca.gov/const-toc.html

Demographic data:
    www.dof.ca.gov/research/demographic
    http://quickfacts.census.gov/qfd/states/06000.html

Digitized photographs, documents, newspapers, political cartoons, works of art, diaries, oral histories, advertising, and other cultural artifacts:
    www.calisphere.universityofcalifornia.edu

LEARN MORE AT THE LIBRARY

Sandra Bass and Bruce M. Cain, eds. *Racial and Ethnic Politics in California*. Berkeley: Berkeley Public Policy Press, Institute of Governmental Studies, University of California, 2008.

Larry N. Gerston. *Not So Golden After All: The Rise and Fall of California*. Boca Raton: CRC Press, 2012.

Joe Matthews and Mark Paul. *California Crackup: How Reform Broke the Golden State and How We Can Fix It*. Berkeley: University of California Press, 2010.

Frank Norris. *The Octopus*. New York: Penguin, 1901. A novel of nineteenth-century California.

Kevin Starr. *California: A History*. New York: Modern Library, 2005.

2

✳

California's Political Parties and Direct Democracy

CHAPTER CONTENTS

Political parties are organizations of like-minded individuals and interest groups that set forth public policies based on their political ideology, put forward candidates for public office, provide the candidates with organizational and financial support, and hold them accountable if they are elected. In some states, parties are strong and do all these things effectively. In California, although party loyalty is strong in the state legislature and among a substantial number of voters, parties are weak as organizations and perform none of these functions effectively. History tells us why: the Progressive reformers intentionally weakened political parties in order to rid California of the railroad-dominated political machine. In doing so, they unintentionally made candidate personalities, media manipulation, and fat campaign war chests as important in elections as political parties—and sometimes more so.

The Progressives also introduced **direct democracy**. Through the initiative, referendum, and recall, California voters gained the power to make law and even to overrule elected officials or remove them between elections. The reformers' intent was to empower citizens, but in practice, interest groups and politicians are more likely to use—and sometimes abuse—direct democracy.

Weak parties and direct democracy are fixtures of the state constitution and modern California politics. Some political observers argue that this combination promotes political disarray, governmental gridlock, and voters who are confused or turned off. Others believe that the system reflects political values that eschew structured authority and maximize opportunities for democratic decision making.

THE PROGRESSIVE LEGACY

To challenge the dominance of the Southern Pacific Railroad's political machine, Progressive reformers focused on the machine's control of party conventions, where party leaders nominated their candidates for various offices. Republican reformers scored the first breakthrough in 1908, when they succeeded in electing many antirailroad candidates to the state legislature. In 1909 the reform legislators replaced party conventions with **primary elections**, in which the registered voters of each party choose the nominees. Candidates who win their party's primary in these elections face the nominees of other parties in the November **general elections**. By instituting this system, the reformers ended the machine's ability to pick the candidates.

In 1910 Progressives won the office of governor and majorities in the state legislature. They introduced direct democracy to give policymaking authority to the people. They also replaced the party column ballot—which had permitted bloc voting for all the candidates of a single party by making just one mark—with separate balloting for each office. In addition, Progressive reformers introduced **cross-filing**, which permitted candidates of one party to seek the nominations of rival parties. Finally, the Progressives instituted **nonpartisan elections**, which eliminated party labels for candidates in elections for judges, school board members, and local government officials.

These changes reduced the railroad's control of the political parties, but they also sapped the strength of party organizations. By allowing the voters to circumvent an unresponsive legislature, direct democracy paved the way for interest groups to dominate policymaking. Deletion of the party column ballot encouraged voters to cast their ballots for members of different parties for different offices (split-ticket voting), increasing the likelihood of a divided-party government (see Chapter 7). Nonpartisan local elections made it difficult for the parties to groom candidates and build their organizations at the grassroots level.

Party leaders tried to regain control of nominations by settling on favored candidates before the primary elections. Ultimately, however, such **preprimary endorsements** were also outlawed. In 1959, when Democrats gained control of the legislature for the first time in over forty years, they outlawed cross-filing, which had been disproportionately helpful to Republican incumbents. This marked a return to the system in which candidates file for nomination for their own party only.

PARTY ORGANIZATION—SYSTEM AND SUPPORTERS

Thanks to the Progressive reforms, political parties in California operate under unusual constraints. Although the original reformers have long since departed from the scene, the reform mentality remains very much a part of California's political culture.

The Official Party System

According to state law, political parties qualify to place candidates on the ballot if a number of voters equal to 1 percent of the state vote in the most recent gubernatorial election sign up for the party when they register to vote; alternatively, parties can submit a petition with signatures amounting to 10 percent of that vote. Once qualified, if a party retains the registration of at least 1 percent of the voters or if at least one of its candidates for any statewide office receives 2 percent of the votes cast, that party remains qualified for the next election. By virtue of their sizes, the Democratic and Republican parties have been fixtures on the ballot almost since statehood.

Minor parties, sometimes called **third parties**, are another story. Some have been on the ballot for decades; others have had brief political lives. In the 2010 general election, the American Independent, Green, Libertarian, and Peace and Freedom parties each secured the minimum 2 percent of the vote for one of their statewide candidates, guaranteeing them positions on the ballot in 2012. The total number of parties qualified for the 2012 California ballot, including Democrats and Republicans, was six.

Nonetheless, breaking the hold of the two major political parties has proved difficult. The Democratic and Republican candidates for governor garnered 95 percent of the vote in 2010—slightly less than the 97.7 percent shared by the Democratic and Republican candidates for president in 2012. Among the smaller parties, the Greens have been the most successful at winning elections. They have earned one seat in the state legislature and elected several city and county officials.

California voters choose their party when they **register to vote**, which must be done fifteen or more days before the election. In 2012, 73.1 percent were registered as either Democrats or Republicans, 6.0 percent signed up with the other parties, and 20.9 percent declared themselves independent (officially known as "decline to state")—see Figure 2.1. The independent percentage has more than doubled since 1986, when it was just 9 percent.

For most of its history, California used **closed primary** elections to select the nominees of each party for state elective office and the U.S. Congress. Voters registered with a political party could cast their ballots in the primary only for that party's nominees for various offices. The winners of each party's primary election faced off in the November general election, when all voters were free to cast their ballots for the candidate of any of the parties.

But in 2010, over the strenuous objections of the political parties (another indication of their weakness), voters approved a **"top–two" primary** system

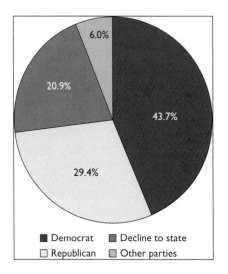

F I G U R E 2.1 Party Registration in California, 2010. (Courtesy of Terry Christensen)

SOURCE: California Secretary of State.

that went into effect in 2012. In a top-two primary, no matter what their own party, voters may choose their preferred candidate from any party; the top-two vote getters face off in the November election, even if they're from the same party. Advocates of this system hoped that instead of concentrating their appeals on the core of their own parties (liberals for Democrats and conservatives for Republicans), candidates would reach out to independent and moderate voters and that those elected would be more moderate and thus more willing to compromise when they got to Sacramento. In theory, this could break the gridlock in the state capital, but whether it will do so remains to be seen.

The June 2012 election was the first statewide top-two primary. The results were mixed and provided few clues about the long-range impact of the new system, although it appears that these elections became somewhat more competitive, which gives voters more choices.[1] For example, significantly more incumbent office holders were confronted by challengers than in the past and more races were close. Not a single minor party candidate made it to the top two, however, which could mean that these parties will eventually disappear under this system. Five "independents" (stating "no party preference" on the ballot) did advance to the November runoff, however. Perhaps most significantly, the top-two primary resulted in twenty-eight runoffs between candidates of the same party. These are the races that the advocates of the top-two primary hope will result in more moderates in the legislature and better prospects for compromise.

Before the Great Depression, California was steadfastly Republican, but during the 1930s a Democratic majority emerged. Since then, Democrats have dominated in voter registration (see Figure 2.2), although their proportion declined from a peak of 60 percent of registered voters in 1942 to 43.7 percent in 2012. Republican registration has slipped to 29.4 percent, while the independent percentage has more than doubled since 1986, when it was just 9 percent. Despite their advantage in registration, Democrats did not gain a majority in

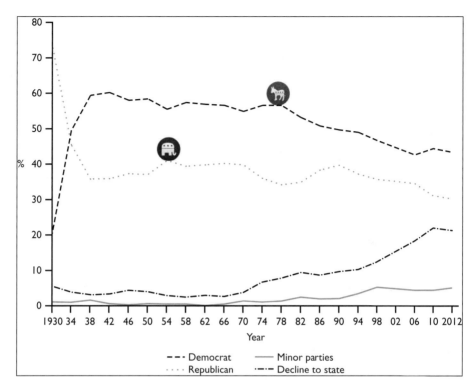

F I G U R E 2.2 Party Registration during Gubernatorial Election Years.
SOURCE: California Secretary of State.

both houses of the state legislature until 1958 and Republican candidates have won eight of the last thirteen gubernatorial elections.

State law dictates registration, voting, and party organization. The main parties have similar structures with the state **central committee** as the highest-ranking body. These committees are comprised of party candidates, office-holders, county chairpersons, and some appointed members. In addition, Democratic voters elect members from each assembly district, and Republican county central committees elect or appoint members. Each party's central committee elects a state chair, who functions as the party spokesperson.

Beneath the state central committee are county central committees. Voters registered with each party choose committee members every two years in primary elections. The party's nominees for state legislature and those who win elections are also members. The state and county party committees draft policy positions for party platforms, although candidates and elected officials often ignore these. Some committees also recruit volunteers and raise money for party candidates. Despite their low public profile, county committees are sometimes sites of intense conflict among activists. Liberals usually dominate Democratic county committees, whereas conservatives rule Republican committees.

California's political parties had an opportunity to strengthen their role in choosing party nominees when the U.S. Supreme Court overturned the state ban on preprimary endorsements in 1990. California Republicans have rarely exercised this power. Democrats have done so more often, although voters don't always pay attention to such endorsements. In 2010, however, the Democratic convention's preprimary endorsement of Assemblyman Dave Jones helped him win the Democratic nomination for state insurance commissioner in an otherwise low-profile race. The influence of such endorsements is limited by the inability of the parties to deliver organizational support to the chosen candidates and by high-spending campaigns and the media, but preprimary endorsements may become more significant with the top-two primary system.

Party Supporters

Besides the official party organizations, a variety of caucuses and clubs are associated with both major parties. The California Republican Assembly is a staunchly conservative statewide grassroots organization that has dominated the Republican Party, thanks to an activist membership. Republican governor Arnold Schwarzenegger, a moderate, had difficulty with the conservatives in his own party. At the 2007 state party convention, he chastised his fellow California Republicans "for their insularity and narrowness," to which they responded "that they'd rather be ideologically principled than pander to moderates."[2] On the Democratic side, liberals dominate through the California Democratic Council, which comprises hundreds of local Democratic clubs organized by geography, gender, race, ethnicity, or sexual orientation.

Party activists such as these are a tiny percentage of the electorate, however. The remaining support base comes from citizens who designate their party affiliations when they register to vote and usually cast their ballots accordingly. Public opinion polls tell us that voters who prefer the Democratic Party tend to be sympathetic to the poor and immigrants; concerned about health care, education, and the environment; in favor of gay rights, gun control, and abortion rights; and supportive of tax increases to provide public services. Those who prefer the Republican Party are more likely to oppose these views and to worry more about big government and high taxes. Of course, many people mix these positions.[3]

Both major parties enjoy widespread support, but the more liberal Democratic Party fares better with blacks, city dwellers, union members, and residents of coastal California and the Sacramento area (see Figure 2.3). Latino voters also favor Democrats, a tendency that was strengthened by Republican support for several statewide initiatives relating to immigration and affirmative action. Voters among most Asian nationalities also lean Democratic, an inclination that has increased in recent years. As with Latinos, Asian interest in the California Republican Party has been weakened by policies and candidates perceived as anti-immigrant. Thanks in large part to the failure of Republicans to win support from minority voters, California is considered a solidly "blue" (Democratic) state, with Democrats holding every statewide office and majorities in the legislature. Unless the Republican party does more to win over minority group voters, demographic trends suggest that the party may be doomed in California.

FIGURE 2.3 California's Partisan Division by County, 2012. (Courtesy of Terry Christensen)

SOURCE: California Secretary of State.

The more conservative Republican Party does better with whites, suburbanites, rural voters, and in Orange County, the Central Valley, and inland California, as well as with older, more affluent voters and with Christian conservatives. These constituencies are more likely to turn out to vote than those that support Democrats, but by 2012, some Republican leaders were worried that the party had declined to such an extent that the advantage in turnout was insufficient. "The California Republican Party has effectively collapsed," declared a prominent Republican political consultant. "It doesn't do any of the things that a political party should do. It doesn't register voters. It doesn't recruit candidates. It doesn't raise money. The Republican Party in the state institutionally has become a small ideological club that is basically in the business of hunting out heretics.... The party is actually shrinking. It's becoming more white. It's becoming older."[4]

In the past, Republican candidates were sometimes successful because they could win the support of Democratic voters thanks to cross-filing (until 1958), charismatic candidates, clever campaigns, and split-ticket voting. But in the 1990s, ticket splitting declined, and instead, voters increasingly voted a straight party-line ticket—either all Democratic or all Republican. This includes decline-to-state voters, who, contrary to common wisdom, are not necessarily independent. Most tilt toward one party or the other, with Democrats enjoying greater support.[5] Some observers assert that the rightward thrust of the Republican Party drove independent voters to the Democrats and was even more important to the Democratic Party's continued success than was winning over minority voters.[6]

DIRECT DEMOCRACY

Voting for candidates is only one way Californians participate in the political process. To counter the railroad machine's control of state and local governments, the Progressive reformers also guaranteed the people a say through the mechanisms of direct democracy: recall, referendum, and initiative. Referenda and initiatives appear on our ballots as "propositions," with numbers assigned by the secretary of state; local measures are assigned letters by the county clerk.

The Recall

The least-used form of direct democracy is the **recall**, which empowers voters to remove officeholders at all levels of government between scheduled elections. Advocates circulate a recall petition with a statement of their reasons for wanting a named official to be removed from office. They must collect a specific number of voter signatures within a specific period. The numbers vary with the office in question. At the local level, for example, the number of signatures required varies from 10 to 30 percent of those who voted in the previous local election; these signatures must be collected over periods that vary between 40 and 160 days. A recall petition for a judge or a legislator requires signatures equaling 20 percent of the vote in the last state election, while for state executive officeholders, the figure is 12 percent. In these cases, petitioners have 160 days to collect the signatures. If enough signatures are collected and validated by the secretary of state (for a state officeholder) or by the county clerk (for a local officeholder), an election is held. The ballot is simple: "Shall [name] be removed from the office of [title]?" The recall takes effect if a majority of voters vote yes, and then either an election or an appointment— whichever state or local law requires—fills the vacancy for the office. Elected officials who are recalled cannot be candidates in the replacement election.

Recalling state officeholders is easier in California than in the other seventeen states where recall is possible. Most other states require more signatures, and while any reason suffices in California, other states require corruption or malfeasance by the officeholder. Nevertheless, recalls are rare in California, where the process is most often used in local government, particularly by parents who are angry with school board members. Even so, only a dozen or so recalls are on local ballots in any given year, and only about half of the officials who face recall are removed from office. Only four state legislators have ever been recalled.

Governor Gray Davis is the only statewide official who had ever been recalled. Davis had barely been reelected in November 2002 when opponents launched a recall petition. Thirty-one previous attempts to recall a California governor had failed to make the ballot, and most political observers assumed that the petitioners would be unable to acquire the 897,158 valid signatures required for an election. They underestimated voter discontent, not only with Davis but also with the general condition of California politics. Davis's decline in popularity resulted from his cautious leadership during the state's energy crisis in 2001, a recession, a huge budget deficit, and the inability of the legislature and the governor to agree on solutions to these problems. An aloof personality also contributed to his troubles. His recall opponents discovered a groundswell of support, facilitated by conservative talk radio hosts and the availability of the Internet to circulate petitions.

In July 2003, the secretary of state certified that 1.3 million valid signatures had been gathered—far more than required—and the election was set for October. Ultimately, 135 candidates qualified to run, including actor Arnold Schwarzenegger. His seventy-five-day campaign took the state by storm, gaining far more media and public attention than any other recent election—thanks in part to his status as a movie star. On Election Day, 55.4 percent of the voters said yes to recall, and Schwarzenegger easily outpaced all other replacement candidates with 48.6 percent of the vote. For the first time in California history—and only the second time ever in the United States—a governor had been recalled.

The Referendum

The **referendum** is another form of direct democracy. A referendum allows the voters to nullify acts of the state government. Referendum advocates have ninety days after the legislature makes a law to collect a number of signatures equal to 5 percent of the votes cast for governor in the previous election (504,760 based on the 2010 vote). Referenda are even rarer than recalls. Of the forty-eight referenda on California ballots since 1912, voters have rejected acts of the government twenty-nine times. A 2004 referendum repealed health-care legislation approved in Governor Davis's last days in office, but in 2012, a referendum that would have repealed a redistricting plan for the state senate failed (see Chapter 5).

The Initiative

Recalls and referenda are reactions to what elected officials do while initiatives allow citizens to make policy themselves by drafting a new law or a constitutional amendment and then circulating petitions to get it onto the ballot. Qualifying a proposed law requires a number of signatures equal to 5 percent of the votes cast for governor in the last election; constitutional amendments require a number of signatures equal to

8 percent (807,615 based on California's 2010 election). If enough valid signatures are obtained within 150 days, the initiative goes to the voters at the next election or, on rare occasions, in a special election called by the governor. As of 2012, all initiatives are on the November general election ballot only—a move advocated by Democrats because voter turnout is higher in November than in June primary elections. This means that more people participate in these decisions, but it also assures maximum turnout of Democratic voters (see Chapter 3).

The subjects of initiatives vary wildly and are often controversial. In the past, voters have approved limits on bilingual education, banned same-sex marriage, and set standards for the size of chicken cages. Other recent propositions have dealt with tribal gambling (repeatedly), redistricting (repeatedly), DNA sampling, and mental health services. In 2012 voters considered several tax measures, the death penalty, punishment for human (sex) trafficking—and more.

Twenty-three other states provide for the initiative, but few rely on it as heavily as California. Relatively few initiatives appeared on ballots until the 1970s, however (see Table 2.1). Then political consultants, interest groups, and governors rediscovered the initiative, and ballot measures proliferated. The 1988 and 1990 election year ballots witnessed an explosion, with eighteen initiatives on each. In 2012 voters faced a total of twelve initiatives in the primary and general elections.

Legislative Initiatives, Constitutional Amendments, and Bonds

Propositions can also be placed on the ballot by the state legislature. Such **legislative initiatives** can include new laws that the legislature prefers to put before the voters rather than enact on its own, or proposed **constitutional amendments**, for which voter approval is compulsory. The 2010 top-two primary measure, for example, was

TABLE 2.1 The Track Record of State Initiatives

Time Period	Number	Number Adopted	Rejected
1912–1919	31	8	23
1920–1929	34	10	24
1930–1939	37	10	27
1940–1949	20	7	13
1950–1959	11	1	10
1960–1969	10	3	7
1970–1979	24	7	17
1980–1989	52	25	27
1990–1999	50	20	30
2000–2009	65	20	45
2010–2012	23	9	14
Total	357	120 (33.6%)	237 (66.4%)

SOURCE: California Secretary of State.

put on the ballot by the legislature as part of a deal to win the vote of a Republican senator for the proposed budget.

Voter approval is also required when the governor or the legislature seeks to issue **bonds** (borrowing money) to finance parks, schools, transportation, or other infrastructure projects. Few of these proposals are controversial, and more than 60 percent pass with minimal campaigning or spending. In the 2006 and 2008 elections, voters approved $29 billion in bonds for projects ranging from high-speed trains to aid for veterans.

THE POLITICS OF BALLOT PROPOSITIONS

The proliferation of ballot propositions is hardly the result of a sudden surge in citizen action. Rather, it stems largely from the opportunism of special interests, individual politicians, and public relations firms. Hundreds of millions of dollars have been spent on ballot measures regulating casinos on Native American lands, the most recent of which appeared on the ballot in 2008. In 2010, Pacific Gas and Electric and Mercury Insurance single-handedly funded separate initiatives that were clearly in their self-interest. They were defeated, but Mercury Insurance came back with another initiative in 2012.

Although intended as mechanisms for citizens to shape policy, even the most grassroots-driven initiatives cost half a million dollars to qualify and millions more to mount a successful campaign. "If you pay enough," declared Ronald George, then chief justice of the California Supreme Court, "you can get anything on the ballot. You pay a little bit more and you get it passed."[7] The campaigns for and against the 2008 proposition banning same-sex marriage spent a total of $83 million—much of it coming from out of state, because California is often seen as setting precedents for campaigns elsewhere. Pacific Gas and Electric spent $43 million on its losing 2010 initiative, while tobacco companies spent $66 million in 2006 and $47 million in 2012 defeating initiatives that would have increased tobacco taxes. Total spending for campaigns for or against propositions in any given election year now averages nearly $300 million. Much of it comes from corporations and unions. According to the California Fair Political Practices Commission, "The conclusion is inescapable: A handful of special interests have a disproportionate amount of influence on California elections and public policy."[8]

Besides wealthy individuals such as business magnate Charles Munger (advocating redistricting reform) and high-tech executive Tim Draper (a supporter of school vouchers), politicians also use initiatives to further their own careers or shape public policy. In 1994, Republican governor Pete Wilson sponsored a successful measure on illegal immigration that helped him win re-election. Movie star Arnold Schwarzenegger sponsored a 2002 initiative to fund after-school programs that launched his political career. As governor, he tried to use ballot measures to further his agenda when thwarted by the Democratic majority in the legislature, but his efforts at political and budget reform were rejected by the voters. In 2012, however, Governor Jerry Brown sponsored an initiative to increase state revenues and won voter approval.

Others also take advantage of direct democracy. Public relations firms and **political consultants**, virtual "guns for hire," have developed lucrative careers managing initiative and referenda campaigns; they offer expertise in public opinion polling, computer-targeted mailing, and television advertising—the staples of modern campaigns. Some firms generate initiatives themselves by conducting test mailings and preliminary polls in hopes of snagging big contracts from proposition sponsors. With millions of dollars in campaign spending hanging in the balance, big economic interests gain an advantage over grassroots efforts—surely not what the Progressives intended.

Nevertheless, direct democracy offers hope to those out of power by enabling them to take their case to the public. Stymied by Democratic dominance of the state legislature for so long, conservatives and business interests have often resorted to the initiative process to pursue their agendas, especially regarding taxes (see Chapter 8). Grassroots groups have also won initiative battles in recent years, including funding mental health programs by increasing taxes on the rich and regulating the treatment of farm animals, despite the strong opposition of agribusiness. In 2012 consumers and organic farmers got a proposition requiring labeling genetically engineered foods on the ballot but were defeated by big-spending opponents. Almost every California ballot includes initiatives generated by grassroots groups. Although these measures are often defeated by well-funded corporate interests, at least direct democracy provides such groups an opportunity to make their cases.

Unfortunately, direct democracy does not necessarily result in good laws. Because self-interested sponsors draft initiatives and media masters run campaigns, careful and rational deliberation is rare. Flaws or contradictions in successful initiatives may take years to resolve. This may be done in the process of implementation or through the legislative process. Sometimes the issue goes back to the voters with successor initiatives. Increasingly, however, disputes about initiatives are resolved in state and federal courts, which must rule on whether the initiatives are consistent with other laws and with the state and federal constitutions. In recent years, courts have overturned all or parts of initiatives dealing with illegal immigration, campaign finance, and same-sex marriage (see Chapter 6). Although such rulings seem to deny the will of the voters, the electorate cannot make laws that contradict the state or federal constitutions.

The increased use of direct democracy has also had an impact on the power of our elected representatives. Although we expect them to make policy, their ability to do so has been constrained by initiatives in recent decades. This is particularly the case with the state budget, much of which is dictated by past ballot measures rather than the legislature or the governor.

The proliferation of initiatives, expensive and deceptive campaigns, flawed laws, and court interventions have annoyed voters and policymakers alike. Perhaps as a consequence, two-thirds of all initiatives are rejected (see Table 2.1). Although Californians express anger and frustration with volume of initiatives they face and the expensive and often confusing campaigns, opinion polls report a solid majority in support of direct democracy in concept.[9]

POLITICAL PARTIES AND DIRECT DEMOCRACY

Authors Mark Baldassare and Cheryl Katz argue that California has evolved into a unique "hybrid democracy," with power divided between elected representatives and the public.[10] Partisan gridlock in Sacramento, voter distrust, and powerful interest groups (see Chapter 4) have resulted in the increased reliance on direct democracy to resolve issues, albeit often imperfectly. California's political parties can't break the gridlock or even control the choice of their own candidates in an electoral system in which money seems to trump party organization. Once elected, our officials seem unable to resolve the issues that confront us. Direct democracy provides an alternative—for political leaders, moneyed interests, and citizens—yet the proliferation of propositions further confounds voters. Does California have too much democracy? Sometimes it seems so. Some voters feel overwhelmed and turned off, but most manage to sift through complex initiatives and seductive campaigns to find the candidates and policies that suit their preferences.

NOTES

1. Public Policy Institute of California, "California's New Electoral Reforms: How Did They Work?" *Just the Facts*, June 2012, www.ppic.org (accessed August 3, 2012).

2. Peter Schrag, "On Race and Gender, the GOP's Tent Is Teeny," *Sacramento Bee*, September 19, 2007.

3. See Public Policy Institute of California, "California Voter and Party Profiles," *Just the Facts*, August 2011, www.ppic.org (accessed August 3, 2012).

4. Adam Nagourney, "In California, G.O.P. Fights Steep Decline," *New York Times*, July 23, 2012.

5. Edward L. Lascher, Jr., and John L. Korey, "The Myth of the Independent Voter, California Style," *California Journal of Politics and Public Policy* 3, no. 1, 2011.

6. Morris P. Fiorina and Samuel J. Abrams, "Is California Really a Blue State?" in *The New Political Geography of California*, ed. Frederick Douzet, Thad Kousser, and Kenneth P. Miller (Berkeley: Berkeley Public Policy Press, Institute of Governmental Studies, University of California, 2008).

7. Ronald George, "Promoting Judicial Independence," *Commonwealth*, February 2006, p. 9.

8. California Fair Political Practices Commission, *Big Money Talks*, March 2010, www .fppc.ca.gov/reports/Report38104.pdf (accessed August 6, 2012).

9. The Field Poll #2394, October 13, 2011.

10. Mark Baldassare and Cheryl Katz, *The Coming Age of Direct Democracy* (New York: Rowman & Littlefield, 2008).

LEARN MORE ON THE WEB

Polling data, including archives:
    www.field.com/fieldpoll or "Statewide Survey," www.ppic.org

California's political parties:
    American Independent Party: www.aipca.org
    California Democratic Party: www.cadem.org
    California Republican Party: www.cagop.org
    Green Party of California: www.cagreens.org
    Libertarian Party of California: www.ca.lp.org
    Peace and Freedom Party: www.peaceandfreedom.org

Elections and ballot measures:
    Ballotpedia: www.ballotpedia.org/
    California Voter Foundation: www.calvoter.org
    California Secretary of State: www.sos.ca.gov/elections/elections_j.htm
    League of Women Voters: www.smartvoter.org and www.easyvoterguide
    .org/

LEARN MORE AT THE LIBRARY

John Allswang. *The Initiative and Referendum in California, 1897–1998.* Stanford, Calif:
    Stanford University Press, 2000.

Center for Government Studies. *Democracy by Initiative.* 2d ed. 2008. www.cgs.org
    (accessed August 6, 2012).

Larry N. Gerston and Terry Christensen, *Recall! California's Political Earthquake.* Armonk,
    N.Y.: M. E. Sharpe, 2004.

GET INVOLVED

Volunteer or intern for a political party. Contact your local county party offices.

3

✳

California Elections, Campaigns, and the Media

CHAPTER CONTENTS

A typical California ballot requires voters to make decisions about more than twenty elective positions and propositions. Even the best-informed citizens sometimes find it difficult to choose among candidates for offices they know little about and to decide on obscure and complicated propositions. Political party labels provide some guidance, but candidates, campaigns, and the media are also crucial in the California elections.

Campaigns and the media are especially important because of the mobility that characterizes California society. More than half of all Californians were born elsewhere, and many voters in every California state election are participating for the first time. Residents also move frequently within the state, reducing the political influence of families, friends, and peer groups and boosting that of campaigns and the media.

THE VOTERS

California citizens who are eighteen years or older are eligible to vote unless they are convicted felons or in mental institutions. Those eligible must **register to vote** at least fifteen days before an election by completing a form available at post offices, fire stations, libraries, and public places where party activists solicit new voters. Registration forms are also available with applications for driver's licenses and at social service agencies or online at www.sos.ca.gov/elections/elections_vr.htm.

Altogether, nearly 23.7 million Californians are eligible to vote. Only 17.1 million (72.3 percent) were registered in 2012, however, and many of those who are registered don't vote. In the gubernatorial election of 2010, only 59 percent of registered voters participated. Turnout is higher in presidential elections. In 2008, 79.4 percent of the state's registered voters participated, although turnout slipped to just 71.3 percent in 2012 election. Far fewer voters participate in June primary elections, however—only 33.3 percent in the 2010 gubernatorial primary and 31 percent in the 2012 presidential primary.

Traditionally, voters go to designated polling places to cast their ballots, but today about half **vote by mail**, having signed up to do so when they register to vote so that ballots are automatically sent to them for every election.

Most of these people simply prefer the convenience of voting by mail given their busy lives; many prefer to deal with the complex ballots at their leisure; and still others vote absentee because campaigns push identified supporters to vote by mail to ensure their participation. With so many more people voting by mail—up to three weeks before Election Day—campaigns have had to change tactics. Rather than a big push in the last few days before the election, they must spread their resources over a longer period.

Voting by mail may have increased participation slightly, but even with this convenience, many Californians choose not to vote. Some don't get around to registering. Millions more who are registered still don't vote. Some are apathetic, some are unaware, and others feel uninformed. Still others believe that voting is a charade because politics "is controlled by special interests." Some people say election information is "too hard to understand," and others are bewildered by all the messages that bombard them during a typical California election. But the reason that people most frequently give for not voting is that they are too busy.[1]

Yet political campaigns are designed to motivate voters to support candidates and causes. This task is complicated, though, because those who vote are not a representative cross-section of the actual population. Non-Latino whites, for example, make up 40 percent of California's population but 66 percent of likely voters. Although Latinos, African Americans, and Asians constitute 60 percent of the state's population, they are only 34 percent of the voters in general elections.[2] This disparity in turnout means that California's voting electorate is not representative of the state's population. The lower participation rate among Latinos and Asians is partly explained by the relative youth of these populations (about one-third of Latinos, for example, are too young to vote) and by the fact that many are not yet citizens.

Language, culture, and socioeconomic status may also be barriers to registration and voting among minority groups. This situation is changing, however;

Latinos were just 8 percent of the state's registered voters in 1978 but are over 20 percent today, and the number continues to rise. Still, voter registration lags among Latino citizens, who comprise an astounding 59 percent of all unregistered voters in California.[3]

Differences in the levels of voter participation do not end with ethnicity. The people most likely to vote are suburban homeowners and Republicans, who tend to be richer, better educated, and older. Lower levels of participation are usually found among poorer, less educated, and younger inner-city residents and Democrats.

According to recent reports, 44 percent of likely voters in California are over the age of fifty-five although this group is 29 percent of the state population, while adults aged eighteen to thirty-four are 33 percent of the population and only 18 percent of likely voters.[4] All this adds up to a voting electorate that is more conservative than the population as a whole, which explains how Republicans sometimes win statewide elections despite the Democratic edge in registration and why liberal ballot measures often fail.

Of course, voting is only one form of political participation. Many people sign petitions, attend public meetings, write letters or e-mails to officials, and contribute money to campaigns. But as we see in Figure 3.1, the number participating diminishes with each form of engagement, and differences among ethnic groups

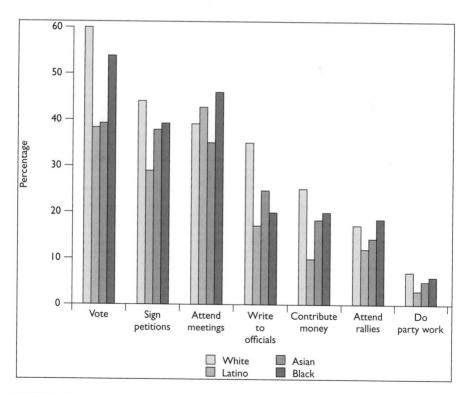

FIGURE 3.1 Political Participation by Ethnic Groups.

SOURCE: From Public Policy Institute of California, "The Ties That Bind," 2004. Reprinted with permission.

persist. As with voting, those who participate most are white, older, more affluent, homeowners, and more highly educated. Does the differential in voting and other forms of participation matter? It seems self-evident that elected officials pay more attention to the concerns of those who participate than those who do not.

THE CANDIDATES

When we vote, we choose among candidates, but where do candidates come from? Some are encouraged to run by political parties or interest groups seeking to advance their causes. Political leaders looking for allies recruit others, although weak political parties make such overtures less common in California than elsewhere. Most California candidates are self starters with an interest in politics who just decide to run and then seek support. The rising cost and increasing negativity of campaigns have discouraged some people from running, although wealthy individuals who can fund their own campaigns have frequently appeared as candidates in recent years. Most candidates start at the bottom of the political ladder, running for school board or city council, and work their way up, building support as they go. Others gain experience as staff members for elected officials, eventually running for their boss's job. Wealthy candidates sometimes skip such apprenticeships and run directly for higher office, but the voters are often skeptical about their lack of political experience.

Historically, candidates in California have been even less representative of the population than the electorate. Most have been educated white males of above-average financial means. The 1990s brought change, however. Underrepresented groups such as women, racial and ethnic minorities, and gay men and lesbians grew in strength and organization, and structural changes facilitated their candidacies. **Term limits** restricting the number of times legislators could be re-elected were introduced, thus ensuring greater turnover in the state legislature. In addition, **redistricting** after the censuses of 1990 and 2000 resulted in redrawn legislative and congressional districts that gave minority candidates new opportunities at both levels. The redistricting that followed the 2010 census continued that trend.

Latinos have gained the most from these changes, electing a significant number of state legislators and members of Congress. Latinos have also gained representation at the local level, electing more than 1,300 of California's county supervisors, city council members, mayors, and school board members.[5] Most Latino officeholders are Democrats.

Although a smaller minority, African Americans gained a foothold in state politics earlier, including the statewide positions of lieutenant governor and superintendent of public instruction. California Attorney General Kamala Harris is African American, Asian, and Native American. Black representation in the state legislature has shrunk, however, as that of other minorities has increased and California's African American population has not grown proportionately.

Asian Americans remain the most underrepresented of California's racial minorities. In the past, Asian Americans have won election to statewide offices, including U.S. senator, secretary of state, and state treasurer. John Chiang, a

Democrat of Chinese descent, was elected state controller in 2006 and re-elected in 2010. Electing candidates has been difficult for Asian Americans, however, because many are recent immigrants who are not yet rooted in the state's political system and because there are cultural and political differences among the Chinese, Japanese, Vietnamese, Koreans, Indo-Americans, and others. But these groups have generated more candidates in every recent election. Many Asians now serve on city councils and school boards, and ten are members of the state legislature.

Women candidates have been more successful. Both of California's U.S. senators as well as its secretary of state and attorney general are women and San Francisco's Nancy Pelosi is the minority leader of the U.S. Congress. A substantial number of women are state legislators and many of California's city council members, mayors, and county supervisors also are women.

Lesbians and gay men achieved elected office later than any of these groups. Greater bias may be a factor, and in the past, the closeted status of homosexual candidates and elected officials weakened organizing efforts and made gay and lesbian elective successes invisible. Nevertheless, over one hundred openly gay and lesbian individuals have won election to local offices (including twenty judges),[6] and seven serve in the state legislature. John Perez, a gay legislator from Los Angeles, holds the powerful position of Speaker of the Assembly.

Racism and sexism partly explain the underrepresentation of all these groups, but other factors contribute as well. Many members of these groups are economically disadvantaged, which makes it hard to participate in politics, let alone to take on the demands of a candidacy. Women, minorities, and gay men and lesbians are usually not plugged in to the network of lobbyists, interest groups, and big donors that provide funds for California's expensive campaigns. Minorities also have difficulty winning support outside their own groups and may alienate their natural constituencies in the process. The fact that minorities are less likely to vote than whites further reduces their candidates' potential. Nevertheless, organizations within each of these constituencies work to recruit, train, and support candidates, and the diversity of California candidates and elected officials increases with each election.

THE MONEY

The introduction of primary elections in 1909 shifted the focus of campaigns from political parties to individual candidates. Political aspirants must raise money, recruit workers, research issues, and plot strategy on their own or with the help of expensive consultants rather than with that of political parties, which contribute little in the way of money or staff.

Weak parties mean that candidates must promote themselves, so the cost of running for state assembly or senate often exceeds $1 million. Spending on races for the legislature totaled over $100 million in the 2009–2010 election cycle. Campaigns for statewide offices are even more expensive. Over $254 million was spent on the race for governor in 2010.[7]

Interest groups, businesses, and wealthy individuals provide the money. Much campaign financing is provided by **political action committees (PACs)**, which interest groups use to direct money to preferred campaigns. Legislative leaders such as the speaker of the assembly and the president pro tem of the senate raise huge sums from such sources and channel the money to their allies; individual candidates raise money by asking potential contributors for donations directly and by organizing special fund-raising events, which range from barbecues to banquets and concerts. They also solicit contributions through targeted mailings and the Internet.

Some wealthy candidates finance their own campaigns. Arnold Schwarzenegger provided more than $10 million for his campaigns in 2003 and 2006, but Republican Meg Whitman broke state and national records by spending $142 million of her own money on her campaign for governor in 2010. Voters are skeptical about wealthy candidates who self-finance their campaigns, however, and in the past, most such candidates, including Whitman, have lost.

Concerned about the influence of money and turned off by campaign advertising, Californians have approved a series of initiatives aimed at regulating campaign finance. The **Political Reform Act of 1974** required public disclosure of all donors and expenditures through the **Fair Political Practices Commission (FPPC)**. In 2000, voters approved **Proposition 34**, a legislative initiative setting contribution limits for individuals and committees (see Table 3.1).

Proposition 34 also set voluntary spending limits for candidates (see Table 3.2). Those who accept the limits have their photo and candidate statements published in the official ballot booklets that go to all voters; candidates who decline the limits are excluded 'from the booklet. Most candidates for the

T A B L E 3.1 Proposition 34 Limits on Contributions to State Candidates, 2011–2012

Contributor	Legislature	Statewide except Governor	Governor
Person	$3,900	$ 6,500	$26,000
Small contributor committee	$7,800	$13,000	$26,000
Political party	No limit	No limit	No limit

SOURCE: California Fair Political Practices Commission, www.fppc.ca.gov.

T A B L E 3.2 Voluntary Expenditure Ceilings for Candidates for State Offices, 2011–2012

Office	Primary	General Election
Assembly	$520,000	$909,000
Senate	780,000	1,169,000
Governor	7,795,000	12,992,000
Other statewide offices	5,179,000	7,795,000

SOURCE: California Fair Political Practices Commission, www.fppc.ca.gov.

legislature and statewide offices other than governor comply with the spending limits; those who do not lose the moral high ground to those who do, which may influence voters. There is no limit, however, on how much a candidate can contribute to his or her own campaign, which enables candidates such as Whitman to substantially fund their campaigns.

Like most reforms, Proposition 34 has had unintended consequences. Money is given to political parties to spend on behalf of candidates rather than to the candidates themselves. More significantly, the new spending limits have been subverted by **independent expenditures** by PACs or groups specially organized by political consultants in support of candidates. Independent spending topped $82 million in California's 2010 elections, including over $45 million for the candidates for governor. Jerry Brown, the victor, was the primary beneficiary. Top independent expenditure groups include the Chamber of Commerce, the California Teachers Association, and other union groups.[8] In some campaigns, independent expenditures exceed those of the candidates. Such spending increased exponentially after the U.S. Supreme Court ruled that the First Amendment prohibited government limits on independent expenditures by unions and corporations in 2010. The only restriction on independent expenditures is that they cannot be coordinated with the campaigns of the candidates they support. Because they are not directly associated with the candidates, "independent" mailings and television ads often feature the most vicious attacks on opponents.

Between independent expenditures, PACs with names that cloak their real purpose and backers (the "Senior Advocates League" was funded by business interests rather than senior groups), and PACs that contribute to other PACs to obscure the individuals and interests who are actually funding campaigns, tracking this information—to "follow the money"—has become ever more complex and difficult. Proposition 34 regulations have been condemned as "ineffective" and even cynically deceptive "reforms."[9] Meanwhile, groups like Common Cause continue to seek ways to limit the role of money in politics.

CAMPAIGNING CALIFORNIA STYLE

Campaign contributors hope to elect allies who will support their interests and expect their money to buy ready access and long-term influence. Candidates deny making specific deals, however, insisting that they and their contributors merely share views on key issues. Millions of dollars flow into candidates' coffers through this murky relationship. In the 2010 election, for example, labor unions generously supported Democrat Jerry Brown, while business interests gave to Meg Whitman.

So much money is needed because California campaigns, whether local or statewide, are highly professionalized. Unable to count on the political parties for funds and support, candidates hire political consultants to recruit workers, raise money, conduct public opinion polls, design advertising, and perform virtually all other campaign activities. These specialists understand the behavior of California voters and use their knowledge to a candidate's benefit.

Television has made campaign management firms indispensable, allowing candidates instant entry into voters' homes. It also enables candidates to put their message across at the exact moment of their choosing—on broadcast or cable TV, between wrestling bouts, during the local news or *Oprah*, or just after *American Idol*, depending on the targeted audience. The efficacy of the medium is proved repeatedly when relatively unknown candidates spend big money on television commercials and become major contenders, as eBay billionaire Meg Whitman did when she saturated the airwaves beginning in late 2009 in the 2010 race for governor. A statewide advertising buy on television may cost $1 million—and one round of ads is never enough.

More than in smaller, more compact states where people are more connected, Californians rely heavily on television for political information. As a consequence, television advertising accounts for a majority of all spending for statewide races in California. In such a big state, it is the only way to reach the mass of voters. At the height of the gubernatorial campaigns, candidates run hundreds of ads a day in California's major media markets. Well-funded initiative campaigns also rely almost exclusively on television advertising, sometimes very effectively. In 2012, an initiative increasing the tax on cigarettes was overwhelmingly supported by the public until the tobacco industry poured $50 million into a confusing and deceptive television ad campaign against the tax and the measure narrowly failed.

Television is too costly for most candidates for legislative and local offices, however. A thirty-second prime-time spot can cost over $20,000 in Los Angeles, and because most television stations broadcast to audiences much larger than a legislative district, the message is wasted on many viewers. Advertising during the day or on cable is cheaper, however, and many legislative candidates have turned to these alternatives. Most, however, have found a more efficient way to spend their money: **direct mail**. Computers have revolutionized political mail by enabling campaign strategists to target selected voters with personal messages.

Direct-mail experts develop lists of voters and their characteristics and then send special mailings to people who share particular qualities. In addition to listing voters by party registration and residence, these experts compile data banks that identify various groups, including liberals and conservatives, ethnic voters, retired people, homeowners and renters, union members, women, gay men and lesbians, and those most likely to vote. Campaigns even do data mining on consumer interests that might predict the political or policy concerns of voters so their mailing can be microtargeted. Once the targets have been identified, campaign strategists can develop just the right message to send to them. Conservatives may be told of the candidate's opposition to gay marriage; liberals may be promised action on the environment. For the price of a single thirty-second television spot, local or legislative candidates can send multiple mailings to their selected audiences.

Television and direct mail dominate California campaigns because they reach the most voters, but the use of these media is not without problems. Because television and direct mail are expensive, campaign costs have risen, as has the influence of major donors. Candidates who are unable to raise vast sums of money are usually left at the starting gate. Incumbent officeholders, who are masters at fund-raising and are well connected to major contributors, become invincible. Furthermore, these media are criticized for oversimplifying issues and emphasizing the negative. Television commercials for ballot measures reduce complicated issues to emotional thirty-second spots aimed at uninformed voters. Candidates' ads and mailings indulge in the same oversimplification, often in the form of attacks on opponents. When the candidates portray each other negatively, voters may feel that they must choose the lesser evil rather than make a decision on the policies and positive traits of the candidates. Voters have grown skeptical of such attacks, yet they are hard to resist and campaign consultants, who are usually blamed for the phenomenon, are certain that the public pays more attention to negative messages than to positive ones.

Candidates also take their campaigns to the Internet, with Web sites and e-mail lists to communicate with the media and with supporters. Campaigns have targeted e-mails to particular constituencies, such as Christian conservatives, and used the Internet to recruit volunteers and solicit donations. The political impact of Internet campaigning is unclear, however. Whereas television and mail enable candidates to reach us whether we're interested or not, the voters themselves must usually initiate contact on the Internet, which limits the audience to those who are already engaged. Campaigns are mining data on Internet users, however, and developing ways to identify potential supporters and get messages and even ads to them online. Interest groups also use e-mail to send campaign messages and mobilize their members.

Overall, California's media-oriented campaigns reinforce both the emphasis on candidates' personalities and voter cynicism. Some people blame such campaigns for declining voter turnout. Contemporary campaigns may also depress voter turnout by aiming all their efforts at regular voters and ignoring those who are less likely to vote—particularly minority or young voters. Although this is a sensible way to use campaign resources, it is not a way to stimulate democracy.

Some candidates try to revive old-fashioned door-to-door or telephone campaigns and get-out-the-vote drives on Election Day. Labor union volunteers have become a force in elections in Los Angeles and San Jose, for example, and the Democratic and Republican parties rely on volunteers to turn out voters for their candidates. Grassroots campaigns have a long and honorable tradition in California, but even in small-scale, local races, they are often up against not only big-money opponents but also the California lifestyle: few people are at home to be contacted, and those who are may let calls go to voice mail or be mistrustful of strangers at their door. For good or ill, candidates need money for their campaigns; those with the most money don't always win, but those with too little rarely even become contenders.

THE NEWS MEDIA AND CALIFORNIA POLITICS

From candidates and campaigns to public policy, almost everything Californians know about politics—which is not necessarily very much—comes from the news media. They have a profound impact on ideas, issues, and leaders. Until the

1950s, a few family-owned newspapers dominated the media. Then television gave the newspapers some competition while expanding the cumulative clout of the mass media. Today, new media like the Internet and a plethora of ethnic publications also play a role.

Paper Politics

California's great newspapers were founded in the nineteenth century by ambitious men such as Harrison Gray Otis of the *Los Angeles Times*, William Randolph Hearst of the *San Francisco Examiner*, and James McClatchy of the *Sacramento Bee*. These print-media moguls used their newspapers to boost their communities, their political candidates, and their favored causes. Most were like Otis, an ardent conservative who fought labor unions and pushed for growth while making a fortune in land investments. In the heyday of bosses and machines, his *Los Angeles Times* supported the Southern Pacific Railroad's political machine and condemned Progressive leader Hiram Johnson as a demagogue, as did many other newspapers in the state. Other journalists, however, helped found the Lincoln-Roosevelt League and led the campaign for reform.

After the Progressives triumphed over the machine, newspapers continued to play a crucial role in California politics. In Los Angeles, San Francisco, Oakland, San Jose, and San Diego, Republican publishers used the power of the press—on editorial and news pages—to promote their favorite candidates and causes. They were instrumental in keeping Republicans in office long after the Democrats gained a majority of registered voters.

Change came in the 1970s, when most of California's family-owned newspapers became part of corporate chains. The new managers brought in more professional editors and reporters. News coverage became more objective, and opinion was more consistently confined to the editorial pages, which became distinctly less conservative. The main newspaper in San Diego, the *U-T*, is an exception to this change. Under the ownership of a local businessman who often uses the newspaper to advocate his own interests, the *U-T* is conservative and pro-business on both its news and editorial pages, like the newspapers of half a century ago.[10]

All these newspapers are extremely influential in California politics through the way they cover the news and through editorials expressing the opinion of the publisher or, more commonly, an editorial board made up of journalists. Voters often follow editorial recommendations on candidates and issues for lack of alternative sources of advice, especially on lower-profile races and ballot measures. Nevertheless, today's editorial pages are less influential than they once were as the number of newspapers and their circulation have declined.

At one time, there were hundreds of newspapers in California, with several competing with one another in most large cities. Today, less than a hundred survive, and most cities have just one. But that's not the only change. As a result of the loss of readers and advertisers to other media, the surviving newspapers have shrunk in both news coverage and staffing. The *Los Angeles Times*, for example, now employs less than half as many journalists as it did in 1998.[11]

As a consequence of these changes, newspaper coverage of California politics is less extensive than it once was. Newspapers now share reporters or rely on the Associated Press or the *Los Angeles Times*, which still maintains the largest and most respected Sacramento bureau. Other media, including television and the Internet, have become more important to many people.

Television Politics

Public opinion surveys report that 37 percent of Californians say they get most of their news and information about politics from television, with 15 percent citing newspapers, 10 percent radio, and 24 percent the Internet.[12] But television coverage of California politics leaves a lot to be desired.

Before Arnold Schwarzenegger was elected governor, not one of California's television stations, other than those based in Sacramento, operated a news bureau in the state capital. Television news editors avoided state political coverage because they believed that viewers wanted big national stories or local features. The minimal television coverage of state politics—a tiny percentage of newscast time, according to various studies—was mainly drawn from newspaper articles, wire service stories, or events staged by politicians, who struggled to gain any coverage at all. Even candidates for governor had a hard time making local news broadcasts, and most television stations declined to broadcast live candidate debates out of fear of low ratings. Cynics pointed out that if television doesn't provide news coverage, candidates are forced to buy advertising time—on television. As a consequence, candidate ads take up more time than news coverage of campaigns during the nightly news on California television stations—and provide a major source of revenue for the stations.

Nevertheless, television coverage of state politics has improved somewhat in the twenty-first century. A movie star governor and his carefully staged media events brought the cameras back to Sacramento. Coverage also increased with the advent of transmission by satellite vans, which made it easier for television stations to send reporters to cover breaking news and major events "live from the Capitol!" without the necessity of investing in permanent Sacramento bureaus. Ongoing conflict between the Republican governor and Democratic majorities in the legislature added drama, as did the state's persistent budget crisis.

Californians who prefer their politics raw—without reporters or commentary—can watch their government in action on the California Channel, now available on 114 cable systems.

New Media

The traditional print and broadcast media still dominate, but in recent years more alternative sources of news and information have become available to Californians. Nearly seven hundred ethnic broadcasting outlets and publications now serve Californians in Spanish, Vietnamese, Mandarin, and many other languages.[13] Latino newspapers and television and radio stations reach major audiences, especially in Southern California. Many of these ethnic media are virtually obsessed with politics as their communities generate candidates or factional conflict.

Talk radio has also become a political fixture, especially in a state where people spend so much time in their cars. Politics is a hot topic on talk radio, which played a crucial role in stirring up the recall of Governor Gray Davis in 2003.

But the medium with the most spectacular recent impact on politics is the Internet. Access to news and information on the Internet has given audiences exponentially more information and sources and diverted audiences and advertisers from more traditional media, especially newspapers. Thousands of Web sites focus on state or local politics and give citizens direct access to their governments. Blogs by political junkies offer news and opinion and often break stories. Listservs and social networking keep members of traditional interest groups in touch with one another and create whole new communities. Seventy-two percent of Californians have a broadband connection at home and 84 percent regularly use the Internet; 44 percent of Californians cite the Internet as a primary source of political news. Latinos, elders, and lower-income residents are less likely to have access to computers or use the Internet, however, so access is not equally distributed.[14]

ELECTIONS, CAMPAIGNS, AND THE MEDIA

The influence of money and the media is greater in California politics than in most other states. Candidates must organize their own campaigns, raise vast sums of money, and then take their cases to the people by mail and television. Such campaigns are inevitably personality oriented, with substantive issues taking a back seat to puff pieces or attacks on opponents. The media provide a check of sorts, but declining coverage limits its impact.

All of this takes us back to the issue of declining voter turnout. Presidential elections increase turnout, but only momentarily. Turnout in primaries and non-presidential elections is much lower. Could stronger parties, more news coverage, and more substantive, issue-oriented campaigns revive voter participation? Maybe, but campaign consultants and the media say that they are already giving the public what it wants.

NOTES

1. California Voter Foundation, "California Voter Participation Survey," March 2005, www.calvoter.org (accessed August 8, 2012).

2. Public Policy Institute of California, "California's Likely Voters," *Just the Facts*, August 2012, www.ppic.org (accessed August 30, 2012).

3. *Ibid.*

4. *Ibid.*

5. National Association of Latino Elected Officials, "2012 Primary Election: California," www.naleo.org (accessed August 9, 2012).

6. Gay and Lesbian Victory Institute, www.victoryinstitute.org/out_officials/ (accessed August 9, 2012).

7. National Institute on Money in Politics, "California 2010," www.followthemoney .org (accessed August 9, 2012).

8. *Ibid.*

9. Dan Walters, "Proposition 34 Only Gave the Appearance of Reform," *San Jose Mercury News,* June 6, 2010.

10. David Carr, "Newspaper as Business Pulpit," *New York Times,* June 10, 2012.

11. "As Cities Downsize from Two Newspapers to Just One, Some Talk of Zero," *New York Times,* March 12, 2009.

12. Public Policy Institute of California, "Californians' News and Information Sources," *Just the Facts,* November 2010, www.ppic.org (accessed August 10, 2012).

13. Marcelo Ballve et al., *Profiles of Ethnic Media: California's New Civic Communicators* (San Francisco: New California Media, 2002).

14. Public Policy Institute of California, "California's Digital Divide," *Just the Facts,* June 2011, www.ppic.org and The Field Poll, Release #2382, June 27, 2011, www.field.com/fieldpollonline/subscribers/ (both accessed August 10, 2012).

LEARN MORE ON THE WEB

Public opinion polls:
>   Public Policy Institute of California: www.ppic.org
>   The Field Poll: http://field.com/fieldpollonline/subscribers/

Elections, political reform, and campaign finance:
>   California Secretary of State: www.sos.ca.gov
>   California Fair Political Practices Commission: www.fppc.ca.gov
>   California Voter Foundation: www.calvoter.org
>   League of Women Voters: www.ca.lwv.org
>   Smart Voter: www.smartvoter.org
>   National Institute on Money in State Politics: www.followthemoney.org

News on state politics, campaigns, and elections:
>   *California Watch:* www.californiawatch.org
>   *Capitol Weekly:* www.capitolweekly.net
>   *California Report* (radio): www.californiareport.org
>   Rough & Tumble (links to news articles on California politics): www .rtumble.com

Listings of publications and broadcast media in California:
>   ABYZ News Links: www.abyznewslinks.com/uniteca.htm

Blogs—for lively opinion and information on California politics:
>   www.calbuzz.com
>   www.calitics.com (progressive)
>   www.flashreport.org (conservative)

LEARN MORE AT THE LIBRARY

Sandra Bass and Bruce E. Cain, eds., *Racial and Ethnic Politics in California*, (Berkeley: Berkeley Public Policy Press, Institute of Governmental Studies, University of California, 2008).

Greg Mitchell, *The Campaign of the Century: Upton Sinclair's Race for Governor of California and the Birth of Media Politics*. New York: Random House, 1992.

Ethan Rarick, ed. *California Votes: The 2010 Governor's Race*. Berkeley: Berkeley Public Policy Press, Institute of Governmental Studies, University of California, 2012.

GET INVOLVED

Volunteer or intern for a campaign. Search for candidates in your district online with www.aroundthecapitol.com or http://votesmart.org/

Register to vote online at http://www.sos.ca.gov/elections/elections_vr.htm.

4

✳

Interest Groups: The Power behind the Dome

CHAPTER CONTENTS

Many people belong to one or more **interest groups**,—organizations formed to protect and promote the shared political objectives of their members. Existing in all shapes and sizes, interest groups range from labor unions, ethnic organizations, and business associations to student unions, environmental entities, and automobile clubs. Whatever their differences, interest groups seek to influence the actions of public policymakers. Sometimes, they are referred to as "special interests" for the special attention they seek and sometimes receive from public officials.

In California, interest groups have prospered and proliferated, and in some ways become more important than political parties. That's because weak political parties and the state's election system provide a fertile political environment for organized groups to exercise influence. Weak political parties leave candidates dependent on groups for campaign contributions, while direct democracy often enables groups to take their issues directly to the voters, circumventing the legislature and other elected policymakers.

Besides exercising their influence through campaign assistance and direct democracy, interest groups also influence legislators in the lobbies beneath the capitol dome. Some observers view these efforts as assisting the legislative process; others see them as manipulating that process.

THE EVOLUTION OF GROUP POWER
IN CALIFORNIA

Interest group influence is found throughout California's lengthy constitution. In other states, groups gain advantages such as tax exemptions through acts of the legislature, which can be changed at any time. In California, such protections are often written into the constitution, making alteration difficult because constitutional amendments require the approval of the electorate.

Different interests have benefited throughout California's colorful history. In the early days, the mining industry and ranchers dominated the state's public policy environment. From about 1870 to 1910, the Southern Pacific Railroad monopolized California's economy and politics, with incredible control over both of California's major political parties in the state legislature. Land development, shipping, and horse racing interests next dominated the political landscape through the mid-twentieth century, followed by the automobile and defense industries. Agricultural interests have remained strong through all these periods.

These days, banking and service businesses tower over manufacturing, while high-tech industries have surpassed defense and aerospace. Insurance companies, teachers' associations, physicians' and attorneys' groups, and other vocation-related associations also routinely lobby state government. Agribusiness also remains influential, particularly with respect to water policy and land use. Organized labor and business interests—almost always at odds—continue to battle for preeminence with the legislature and voters. They have been joined by the California Nations Indian Gaming Association, the largest contributor to several ballot propositions that have asked the voters to ratify gaming agreements between the tribes and the state. Narrow social issue groups, such as Gun Owners of California and Mothers Against Drunk Driving (MADD), have entered the fray, along with evangelical, pro-choice, right-to-life, minority, feminist, and gay and lesbian groups. Public interest groups, such as the League of Women Voters, Common Cause, and The Utility Reform Network (TURN), are also part of the ever-growing interest group mix. Pressured by these many organizations and their financial contributions, California politicians often find themselves responding to the demands of interest groups rather than governing them.

TYPES OF GROUPS

Interest groups vary in size, resources, and goals. At one extreme, groups with narrow and targeted economic benefits tend to have relatively small memberships but substantial financial resources. At the other end of the spectrum, public interest groups with large memberships tend to have little money. A few, such as the Consumer Attorneys of California (CAC), whose membership consists of 3,000 trial lawyers, have the dual advantage of being both large and well funded. Others, such as the Consumers for Auto Reliability and Safety (CARS), operate on a shoestring. Still others, such as the California Teachers Association and California Chamber of Commerce, have more members paying dues than the state Democratic and Republican parties.

Economic Groups

Economic groups that seek various financial gains or hope to prevent losses dominate the state's interest group environment. Every major corporation in the state, from Southern California Edison to the California Northern Railroad, is represented in Sacramento either by its own lobbyists or by lobbying firms hired to present the corporation's cases to policymakers. Often, individual corporations or businesses with similar goals form broad-based associations to further their general objectives. These umbrella organizations include the California Manufacturers and Technology Association, the California Business Alliance (for small enterprises), the California Bankers Association, and the California Council for Environmental and Economic Balance (for utilities and oil companies). The California Chamber of Commerce alone boasts 16,000 member companies with one-fourth of the state's private sector workforce. Each year the Chamber publishes a list of "job killer" bills under consideration and then produces a report on the final outcome which shows defeat of most of the list either by the legislature or governor's veto. In 2011, the Chamber was successful on eleven of twelve bills it opposed.

Agribusiness is particularly active, because farming depends on the government on issues such as water availability and the regulation of pesticides. The giant farming operations maintain their own lobbyists, but various producer groups also form associations. Most of the state's winemakers, for example, are represented by the 1,000-member Wine Institute. The California Cotton Ginners Association has only forty-two members, yet produces 700 million bales of cotton annually. Broader organizations, such as the California Farm Bureau Federation, one of the state's most powerful lobby groups, speak for agribusiness in general by representing 85,000 members with crops in excess of $40 billion in value.

Recently, high-tech industries have asserted their interests on issues ranging from Internet taxation and H-1B visas for foreign workers to transportation and public education. Organizations such as TechNet, the Silicon Valley Leadership Group, and the American Electronics Association have lobbied for regulatory changes, tax relief, research and development tax credits, "green" incentives in new areas such as solar energy, and other changes. The tech-heavy Silicon Valley

Leadership Group alone represents 375 companies that provide $3 trillion worth of services and products in the global economy, exceeding the entire gross domestic product of France.

Professional Associations and Unions

Professional associations such as the California Medical Association (CMA), the California Association of Realtors (CAR), and the Consumer Attorneys of California (CAOC) are among the state's most active groups, and they are regularly among the largest campaign contributors. Other professionals, such as chiropractors, dentists, and general contractors, also maintain active associations. Because all these professionals serve the public, many promote their concerns as broader than self-interest. Their credibility is further enhanced by expertise they possess in their respective fields.

Teachers' associations and other public employee organizations fall somewhere between business associations and labor unions. Their members view themselves as professionals but in recent years have increasingly resorted to traditional labor union tactics, among them collective bargaining, strikes, and political campaign donations. Other public workers, including the highway patrol and state university professors, have their own organizations.

Unions have done well in California, which ranks sixth (tied with Oregon) among the fifty states in per capita union membership. Unions here represent 17 percent of the workforce, compared with 12 percent nationwide. Traditional labor unions represent nurses, machinists, carpenters, public utility employees, and dozens of other occupations. In the past few years, they have persuaded the legislature to enact the nation's first paid family leave program, allowing workers to take leave from their jobs for up to six weeks, and provide paid paternity leave, which also was the first program of its kind in the nation. The laws drew the wrath of the California Chamber of Commerce, which predicted that they would create hardship for businesses, yet only a fraction of those eligible to participate actually do so.[1]

Perhaps the most controversial union in state politics is the California Correctional Peace Officers Association (CCPOA), which contributed more than $600,000 to the reelection campaign of Governor Gray Davis in 2002, just before the governor signed a three-year pay increase of 35 percent in the midst of a huge state budget deficit. The agreement added fuel to the recall accusation that Davis was little more than a tool of major contributors. In 2004 Governor Arnold Schwarzenegger renegotiated the contract and won a slight modification in the pay raises. Still, the CCPOA has persevered its own interests. In 2008 the union funneled $1.8 million into a campaign to help defeat a ballot proposition which would have provided drug treatment and rehabilitation programs for many nonviolent drug offenders who otherwise would be sent to prison.

Demographic Groups

Groups that depend more on membership numbers than on money can be described as **demographic groups**. Based on characteristics that distinguish their members from other segments of the population, such as their ethnicity, gender, or age, such groups usually have an interest in overcoming discrimination. Most racial and ethnic organizations fall into this category.

Virtually all of California's minorities have organizations that represent their voice. One of the earliest was the Colored Convention, which fought for the rights of African Americans in California in the nineteenth century. Today, several such groups advocate for African Americans, Asian Americans, and Native Americans. The United Farm Workers (UFW), GI Forum, Mexican American Legal Defense Fund (MALDEF), and Mexican American Political Association (MAPA) represent Latinos.

The National Organization for Women (NOW), EMILY's List (Early Money Is Like Yeast), and National Women's Political Caucus (NWPC) actively support women candidates and feminist causes. Unlike some of the other statewide organizations, these groups are better organized at the local level than at the state level, however.

Several organizations have become prominent over the definition of sexual equality. Gay rights groups have increased in numbers and voice in recent years, particularly over the issue of gay marriage. Equality California, the largest, has worked to elect gay legislators, obtain passage of equal rights legislation, and pursue gay marriage through both the courts and the legislative process. They have been opposed by groups like Campaign for California Families, which define marriage as a union only between a man and woman.

With California's aging population heavily dependent on public services, this demographic also plays a role in state politics. Organizations such as AARP (formerly the American Association of Retired Persons), with 3 million members in California, have achieved a high profile in state politics, particularly on health-care issues.

Single-Issue Groups

The groups discussed so far tend to have broad bases and deal with a wide range of issues. Another type of interest group operates with a broad base of support for the resolution of narrow issues. **Single-issue groups** push for a specific question to be decided on specific terms. They support only candidates who agree with their particular position on an issue. The California Abortion Rights Action League (CARAL), for example, endorses only candidates who support a woman's right to choose (pro-choice), whereas antiabortion (or pro-life) groups such as the ProLife Council work only for candidates on the opposite side. Likewise, the Howard Jarvis Taxpayers Association evaluates candidates and ballot propositions solely in terms of whether they meet the association's objective of no unnecessary taxes and no wasteful government spending. Antitax groups have been very effective, especially with Republican legislators.

A single-interest group's potential ability to deliver a solid bloc of voters on a controversial issue can affect the outcome of an election and thus enhance its clout, at least on a temporary basis. That's what happened in 1994 when then Republican Governor Pete Wilson sailed to reelection on the tail wind of "Save Our State," an anti-immigrant proposition supported by the California

Coalition for Immigration Reform. An exception occurred in 2008, when anti-gay groups qualified and campaigned heavily for **Proposition 8**, a proposed constitutional amendment designed to overturn a state supreme court decision that had legalized same-sex marriage.[2] Advocates urged voters to use presidential candidate positions on the proposition as a guide to their presidential election votes. Barack Obama opposed the measure, yet he won California handily as the initiative squeaked by.

Public Interest Groups

Although virtually all organized interest groups claim to speak for the broader public interest, some groups clearly seek no private gain and thus more correctly can claim to be **public interest groups**. These groups are distinguished from other organizations by the fact that they pursue goals to benefit society, not just their members.

Some public interest groups, such as California OneCare, have been instrumental in the fight for health-care reform. Others, such as The Utility Reform Network (TURN), monitor rate requests by the utilities before the state Public Utilities Commission. In 2010, TURN led a coalition of consumer groups against a PG&E-sponsored ballot proposition that would have made it very difficult for municipalities to purchase renewable power.

Environmental organizations such as the Sierra Club and Friends of the Earth have been very active in California on water management, offshore oil drilling, air pollution, transportation, and pesticide use. Another important concern of these groups is land use, both for private development in sensitive areas and for public lands, which make up half the state. Surveys have reported that one in nine Californians claims membership in an environmental group.[3] The Sierra Club alone has more than 1.4 million members.

Other public interest groups, such as California Public Interest Research Group (CALPIRG), the California Budget Project, Common Cause, and the League of Women Voters, focus on governmental reform, campaign finance, and voter participation.

A final type of public interest group isn't really a group at all: local governments. Cities, school districts, special districts, and counties all lobby the state government—on whose funds they depend heavily—through the League of California Cities, the California School Boards Association (CSBA), and the California State Association of Counties (CSAC). Dozens of cities and counties employ their own lobbyists in Sacramento, as do other governmental agencies. One study found that local governments collectively spend more on lobbying than do organized labor, oil companies, or businesses.[4] They also endorse ballot measures that affect their interests and, on rare occasions, even sponsor initiatives.

Unlike other groups, cities and counties cannot make campaign contributions, but they can speak out. In 2010, local governments banded together to promote **Proposition 22, the Local Taxpayers, Public Safety and Transportation Act**, an initiative to keep the state government from borrowing or raiding funds that voters have dedicated to public safety.

TECHNIQUES AND TARGETS:
INTEREST GROUPS AT WORK

Interest groups seek to influence public policy. To do this, they must persuade policymakers. The legislature, the executive branch, the courts, the bureaucracy, and sometimes the people are thus the targets of the various techniques these groups may use. Their primary weapons include lobbying, campaign support, litigation, and direct democracy.

Lobbying

The term **lobbying** refers to the activity that once went on in the foyers adjacent to the legislative chambers. Advocates for various causes or issues would buttonhole legislators on their way in or out of the chambers and make their cases. This still goes on in the lobbies and hallways of the capitol, as well as in nearby bars and restaurants and wherever else policymakers congregate. Lobbyists are so integral to the legislative process that they are commonly referred to as members of the "third house," alongside the assembly and senate.

Until the 1950s, lobbying was a crude and completely unregulated activity. Lobbyists lavished food, drink, gifts, and money on legislators in exchange for favorable votes. Today's lobbyists, however, are experts on the legislative process. Many have served as legislators or staff for legislators. Often, they focus on legislative committees and leaders, lobbying the full legislature only as a last resort.

Unlike old-time lobbyists, today's advocates must be well informed to be persuasive. When inexperienced legislators are unable to grasp major issues, lobbyists fill the void, often by actually writing proposed legislation and assembling the coalitions of legislators necessary to pass it. One study during the 2007–2008 legislative session found that 60 percent of the bills that became laws had been introduced by legislators on behalf of lobbyists.[5] Today's lobbyists still use money, but less cavalierly than in the past, instead strategically contributing to campaigns. Legislators and lobbyists alike assert that contributions buy access, not votes, but the tie between money and access can be powerful in its own right. "The bottom line," one strategist states, is that "the system favors the moneyed—and there's been no sign of political reform."[6] All of this makes lobbying not only a highly specialized profession but also an expensive activity. As an example, during the 2011 session, lobby firms spent about $286 million just to influence the legislature alone—up from $151 million in 2009. That averages $2.4 million per legislator.[7]

Although most lobbying activity is focused on the legislature, knowledgeable professionals also target the executive branch, from the governor down to the bureaucracy. The governor not only proposes the budget but also must respond to thousands of bills that await his or her approval or rejection. In the process, the governor frequently meets with lobbyists in an effort to find common ground on proposed legislation.[8]

Bureaucrats also are targets of astute interest groups. The bureaucracy must interpret new laws and make future recommendations to the governor and legislature. Moreover, on questions ranging from tax exemptions to coastal access to energy regulations, bureaucrats often have the final say on how laws will work. One study on the implementation of AB 32, the Global Warming Solutions Act of 2006, found energy interests lobbying the California Air Resources Board more than the governor or legislature to gain favorable regulations. In the words of one lobbyist, "I'm not going to say we love the thing (AB 32), but if that's the way the state wants to go … we want to make sure that we write regulations that we can comply with and are feasible to do."[9] Sometimes lobbyists will go so far as to offer "talking points" to help bureaucrats justify their decisions on public matters. "It's called 'spoon feeding,'" a lobbyist recently explained to a California coastal commissioner regarding a matter before the commission, "but we're happy to do it."[10]

Lately, the public has become a target of lobbying, too. In media-addicted California, groups have begun making their cases through newspaper and television advertising between elections. Health care, education, energy, Indian gaming, and other issues have been subjects of costly media campaigns with the intent to motivate voters to communicate with state leaders.

Professional Lobbyists.   Between 1977 and 2011, the number of registered lobbyists in Sacramento nearly doubled, from 582 to about 1,200, including about fifty former legislators. That's about ten lobbyists per legislator. State law prevents former legislators from lobbying for one year after they leave office, but as one legislator has noted, "I would certainly be available to give people political advice."[11] Even at that, legislators often wait out the transition year by serving as "consultants"—one more example of the blurry connection between those in and out of elected office.

Most lobbyists represent a particular business, union, organization, or group. Others are **contract lobbyists**, advocates who work for several clients simultaneously. Whether contract or specialized, more and more lobbyists make a career of their professions, accruing vast knowledge and experience. These long-term professionals became even more powerful when term limits eliminated senior legislators with countervailing knowledge, although some lobbyists complain that term limits mean they must constantly reestablish their credibility with new decision makers. One prominent lobbyist, however, explains his lack of concern about term limits or other reforms: "Whatever your rules are, I'm going to win."[12]

Nonprofessional Lobbyists.   Some groups can't afford to hire a lobbyist, so they rely on their members instead. Even groups with professional help use their members on occasion to show elected officials the breadth of their support. Typically, this sort of lobbying is conducted by individuals who live in the districts of targeted legislators, although groups sometimes lobby en masse, busing members to the capitol for demonstrations or concurrent lobbying of many elected officials.

Such grassroots efforts by nonprofessionals have special credibility with legislators, but well-financed groups have learned to mimic grassroots efforts by forming front groups or "Astroturf" organizations that conceal their real interests. In 2009, for example, representatives of pornography filmmakers flooded the capitol for hearings on a bill that would have hiked taxes on the industry from 8 percent to 25 percent, adding $665 million to the beleaguered state coffers. Bill opponents included spokespersons from the Free Speech Coalition (FSC), an adult industry-funded group purportedly concerned with government efforts to limit free speech, regardless of the topic or issue. In this case, the FSC representatives argued that the tax would discriminate against those with different opinions. Through this vehicle, the porn industry appeared less self-serving and provided the logic for legislators to defeat the bill.

Campaign Support

Most groups also try to further their cause by helping sympathetic candidates win election and reelection, commonly through financial contributions to their campaigns. Groups with limited financial resources do so by providing volunteers to go door-to-door or to serve as phone-bank callers for candidates. Labor unions typically fall into this category, along with public education interests. Business groups, however, tend to be the most successful in having their way through generous financial support.

Take the issue of consumer protection from cell phone companies. In general, the telecommunications industry has thwarted efforts to make fees transparent, eliminate monthly charges for unlisted numbers, and ease consumer ability to reject phone books according to a recent study.[13] Much of that success is due to the campaign support from AT&T. State records show that between 2004 and 2011, AT&T spent $36.8 million attempting to influence lawmakers three times as much as the next closest company. In 2011 alone, every single member of the legislature received a campaign contribution from the telecommunications giant.[14] Table 4.1 shows the largest campaign contributor groups for 2010.

T A B L E 4.1 Top Ten Campaign Contributor Groups, 2010

Category	Money
Electric utilities	$50,954,029
Public-sector unions	45,763,576
General trade unions	28,928,580
Party committees	25,135,721
Insurance	24,653,667
Candidate committees	22,544,852
Securities & investment	19,885,802
Pro-environmental policy	18,903,579
Oil & gas	18,766,717
Lawyers & lobbyists	14,343,096

SOURCE: Institute on Money in State Politics, www.followthemoney.org.

Campaign contributors claim that their money merely buys them access to decision makers. The press and the public often suspect a more conspiratorial arrangement, however, and evidence of money-for-vote trades has emerged in recent years. In 1994, fourteen people, including five state legislators, were convicted of providing favors in exchange for campaign contributions. In another instance Chuck Quackenbush, California's elected insurance commissioner, was forced to resign in 2000 after he let insurance companies accused of wrongdoing avoid big fines by contributing to foundations that spent the money on ads and other activities featuring the commissioner. And in 2005, Secretary of State Kevin Shelley resigned from his office after several allegations of illegal activities, including campaign contributions from a company that was awarded a major grant from his office.

As a result of these scandals, politicians and contributors probably exercise greater caution. The high cost of campaigning in California, though, means that candidates continue to ask and lobbyists and interest groups continue to give. Of significance, however, is that the campaign funds come from a variety of interest groups, as well as other sources.

Litigation

Litigation is an option when a group questions the legality of legislation, and in recent years many groups have turned to the courts for a final interpretation of the law. Groups have challenged state laws, regulations, and actions by the executive branch in court. In 2010, for example, the California Nurses Association successfully sued to force Governor Arnold Schwarzenegger to comply with a new state law that reduced the nurse-to-patient ratio. Although the governor lost that battle, he won another when he fended off a court challenge by the powerful California Teachers Association because he rescinded an earlier promise to return $2 billion he had denied the schools the previous year.

Over the years, interest groups have also raised legal challenges to several successful ballot measures—including measures on immigration, affirmative action, campaign finance, bilingual education, and same-sex marriage—hoping that the initiatives would be declared unconstitutional. Even if a group loses its case, it may be able to delay the implementation of a new law or at least establish a principle for debate in the future. In 2001 MALDEF challenged the legislature's redistricting plan, claiming under representation of Latinos. Although the legislature's plan prevailed, MALDEF's tactic kept the issue on the public agenda throughout the decade, helping to set the stage for more favorable redistricting consideration in 2011.

Direct Democracy

In his 1911 inaugural address, Governor Hiram Johnson championed direct democracy to "place in the hands of the people the means by which they may protect themselves." He and his fellow Progressives envisioned the public as the ultimate custodian of the legislative process. A century later, however, only broad-based or well-financed groups have the resources to collect the necessary signatures or to pay for expensive campaigns. **Direct democracy** gives interest groups the opportunity to promote their policy proposals through initiatives and referenda.

Sometimes interest groups mobilize to gain passage of a ballot proposition; other times they work to defeat one. In 1998, for example, tribal supporters of gambling on Indian lands spent $10 million qualifying an initiative for the ballot in just thirty days—the most expensive petition drive in history. The subsequent campaign on the proposition itself also broke records, with the two sides spending a total of $96 million. The voters ultimately approved the initiative. Since then, the costs have gone up. In 2008 the voters were asked to ratify four agreements allowing for 17,000 more slot machines in Indian casinos in addition to the 62,000 already in place, providing the state with $450 million in new revenues. The pro-gaming interests spent more than $150 million on campaign activities—far exceeding the "no" side, which spent less than $40 million. The ballot propositions sailed through.

Big money was spent against another initiative in 2012 when the tobacco industry marshaled nearly $50 million against Proposition 29, which sought to increase tobacco taxes by $1.00 per cigarette package. Health and environmental interests were able to raise only $12 million in a losing battle.

But the largest campaign war chests don't always win. For example, utility giant PG&E spent more than $3 million in 2010 gathering signatures for Proposition 16, the so-called Taxpayers Right to Vote Act. The proposal was actually a thinly veiled effort to change the state constitution to require any municipal power company to get a two-thirds vote of the people before buying renewable energy. PG&E poured more than $46 million into the effort against about $90,000 spent by the "no" side. The proposal was defeated, even though the opponents were outspent by a margin of 19,565 to 1.

The recall is also sometimes used by interest groups, usually to remove local elected officials. Teachers' unions, conservative Christians, and minority groups have conducted recall campaigns against school trustees, for example. These efforts, however, pale in comparison with the recall effort against Governor Gray Davis. The People's Advocate, a conservative antitax group, was among the leading forces early in that recall effort. During the campaign, groups ranging from the Howard Jarvis Taxpayers Association to the League of Conservation Voters weighed in on the issue.

REGULATING GROUPS

Free spending by interest groups and allegations of corruption led to the Political Reform Act of 1974 (introduced in Chapter 3), an initiative sponsored by Common Cause. Overwhelmingly approved by the voters, the law requires politicians to report their assets, disclose contributions, and declare how they spend campaign funds. Other provisions compel lobbyists to register with the secretary of state, file quarterly reports on their campaign-related activities, and reveal the beneficiaries of their donations. The measure also established the **Fair Political Practices Commission (FPPC)**, an independent regulatory body, to monitor these activities. When the commission finds incomplete or inaccurate reporting, it may fine the violator. Of greater concern than the financial penalty, however, is the bad press for those who incur the commission's reprimand.

The voters approved new constraints in 1996, when they enacted strict limits on interest groups' practice of rewarding supportive legislators with travel and generous fees for speeches. However, this legislation was soon challenged, creating an atmosphere of uncertainty. In 2000 voters approved yet another initiative which placed new constraints on political action committees and attempted to limit contributions to political campaigns. Yet between self-financed campaigns and the vigorous activities of groups engaged in independent expenditures, any thoughts of reduced spending quickly vanished.

MEASURING GROUP CLOUT: MONEY, NUMBERS, AND CREDIBILITY

Campaign regulations are generally intended to reduce the disproportionate influence of moneyed interests in state politics, but economic groups still have the advantage. Their stable of resources gives them the staying power to outlast the enthusiasm and energy of grassroots groups.

Public interest groups and demographic groups, however, gain strength from numbers, credibility, and motives other than self-interest. Occasionally they prevail, such as in 1998, when children's groups and health groups overcame a financial disadvantage to pass Proposition 10, a cigarette tax dedicated to children's health programs, and in 2010, when financially impotent public interest groups won the Proposition 16 battle against PG&E. More commonly, interest groups affected by potentially harmful new costs rise to the occasion, as was the case in 2006, when the oil and tobacco industries spent nearly $200 million and reversed public opinion—and the votes—on measures to tax oil and increase tobacco taxes.

How powerful are interest groups and their lobbyists? It's hard to tell, but one informal survey of twelve first-time legislators reported that lobbyists wrote 70 percent of the bills they proposed,[20] perhaps reflecting the extent that new legislators are most vulnerable to interest group activity.

Whatever the balance among groups, they are central to California politics. In a political environment characterized by weak political parties and direct democracy, California's myriad interests have plenty of opportunity to thrive.

NOTES

1. *California Business Issues, 2004* (Sacramento: California Chamber of Commerce, 2004), p. 77; also see "Few Take State's Family Leave," *San Jose Mercury News*, July 4, 2006, pp. 1C, 9C.

2. The ruling was *In re Marriage Cases*, S147999.

3. Public Policy Institute of California, *Statewide Survey*, June 2000, www.ppic.org.

4. "Cities, Counties, Pay Price for Capitol Clout," *Los Angeles Times*, September 10, 2007, pp. B1, B4.

5. "How Our Laws Are Really Made," *San Jose Mercury News*, July 11, 2010, pp. A1, A6, A7.

6. "Special Interests: How They Get around Voter-Approved Limits on Campaign Contributions," *San Francisco Chronicle*, February 11, 2008, pp. A1, A6.

7. "Lobbying of Legislators Sets Record," *Los Angeles Times*, March 6, 2012, pp. AA1, AA4.

8. See "A Lobbyist by Any Other Name?" *San Jose Mercury News*, May 20, 2005, pp, 1A, 17A.

9. "Lobbyists Heat Up over Climate Law," *Sacramento Bee*, July 12, 2010, pp. A1, A10.

10. "E-mails Put California Coastal Commissioner in an Awkward Spot," *Los Angeles Times*, July 10, 2010, p. AA3.

11. "Elective Office Improves a Resume," *Los Angeles Times*, November 24, 2006, pp. B1, B11.

12. Douglas Foster, "The Lame Duck State," *Harper's*, February 1994.

13. "Business Interests Have an Edge in Lobbying," *San Francisco Chronicle*, December 26, 2011, pp. A1, A11.

14. "AT&T Is Dialed In to Sacramento," *Los Angeles Times*, April 22, 2012, pp. A1, A17.

15. Foster, *op. cit.*

LEARN MORE ON THE WEB

California Association of Realtors (CAR):
www.car.org

California Chamber of Commerce:
www.calchamber.com

California Labor Federation:
www.calaborfed.org

Common Cause:
www.commoncause.org

Howard Jarvis Taxpayers Association:
www.hjta.org

Latino Issues Forum:
 www.lif.org

League of Women Voters of California:
 www.ca.lwv.org

Sierra Club:
 www.sierraclub.org/ca

LEARN MORE AT THE LIBRARY

Mark Arax and Rick Wartzman. *The King of California*. New York: Public Affairs Press, 2003.

Derek Cressman. *The Recall's Broken Promise: How Big Money Still Runs California Politics*. Sacramento, CA: The Poplar Institute, 2007.

Frank Norris. *The Octopus*. New York: Doubleday and Company, 1901.

Stephanie S. Pincetl. *Transforming California: A Political History of Land Use and Development*. Baltimore, MD: The Johns Hopkins University Press, 1999.

Arthur H. Samish and Bob Thomas. The Secret Boss of California. New York: Crown Books, 1971.

Dan Walters and Jay Michael. *The Third House*. Berkeley: Berkeley Public Policy Press, Institute of Governmental Studies, University of California, 2002.

GET INVOLVED

Volunteer or intern for an interest group in your community—just search on the Internet for the one that interests you.

5

✴

The Legislature: The Perils of Policymaking

CHAPTER CONTENTS

Thousands of bills are passed in the California legislature every year. Some are narrow in focus, such as a law that bans children under eighteen from using tanning beds (passed in 2011). Others are sweeping in impact, like the first-of-its kind Homeowners Bill of Rights (passed in 2012). Some of these laws may seem trivial to the casual observer, but the bottom line is that the legislature is responsible for tackling the state's problems, big and small.

Of course, the legislature does not act in a policymaking vacuum; rather, it must share power with the other branches of government, particularly the executive branch. In addition, the legislature has internal problems to manage, due to political—and philosophical—battles not only between Democrats and Republicans, but also internally between assembly Democrats and senate Democrats and assembly Republicans and senate Republicans. As one beleaguered assembly member once said, "More times than not, it seems that we have four political parties in the legislature alone!" Partisanship and ideological schisms fracture the legislative process in California, and these stark divisions often leave the body tied in political knots.

Then there's the question of public policy priorities. Some observers have wondered in recent years how the legislature could immerse itself in issues such as regulations on imported kangaroo leather and banning shark fins, yet seemingly avoid questions about tax reform, water policy, underfunded public education, and a frayed infrastructure. It's no wonder that a 2012 public opinion survey found a whopping 71 percent of likely voters critical of the state legislature—a disapproval rating nearly twice as high as that for Governor Jerry Brown.[1] Still, the legislature was established as the state institution most directly linking the people with their government. The question is, does it still do its job in the twenty-first century?

THE MAKING AND UNMAKING OF A MODEL LEGISLATURE

Structurally and numerically, much of today's state legislature parallels its original design and intent. But a series of circumstances in the state's political environment have left the legislative branch considerably different than its national counterpart.

A Little History

California's first constitution, in 1849, provided a **bicameral (two-house) legislature** similar to the U.S. Congress. When the constitution was revised thirty years later, the senate was fixed at forty members serving four-year terms (with half the body elected every two years); the assembly was set at eighty members serving two-year terms. Those numbers and terms of office continue to this day. Throughout the first century of governance, legislators met on a part-time basis, with budgets crafted in two-year increments—characteristics that would change over time.

Beginning in 1926, the organization of the legislature paralleled that of the U.S. Congress. Assembly members, like their counterparts in the House of Representatives, were elected on the basis of population, and senators were elected by county in the same way that each state has two U.S. senators.[2] The large number of lightly populated counties north of the Tehachapi Mountains enabled the rural north to dominate the state senate despite Southern California's growth. By 1965, twenty-one of the forty state senators in California represented only 10 percent of the population; Los Angeles County, then home to 35 percent of the state's residents, had but a single state senator.

The Shift toward Professionalism

Then came change. The U.S. Supreme Court's **Reynolds v. Sims** decision in 1964 ordered all states to organize their upper houses by population rather than by county or territory. In California, urban and southern representation increased dramatically, with rural and northern areas experiencing a corresponding decline. The new legislators were younger, better educated, more ideological, and with more varied ethnic and gender backgrounds. The transition to modernity was completed in 1966, when the voters created a full-time legislature with full-time salaries.

These days, the legislature meets an average of more than two hundred days per year, with full-time salaries to match. As of 2013, the legislators' base salary is $90,526, the highest among the fifty states. Perks push annual incomes close to $120,000.[3] Only nine other states have full-time legislatures.[4]

Redistricting: Keeping and Losing Control

By law, every ten years after the national census, the state realigns congressional and state legislative districts to have approximately the same populations. This process is known as **redistricting**. Until 2011, redistricting had been carried out by the legislature, as in most states. Consequently, the partisan composition of the legislature remained almost identical throughout the decade because the districts contained artificially high numbers of Democrats or Republicans, reflecting the parties of the incumbents. For example, after the 2001 redistricting process, one senate district was two hundred miles in length, while others appeared almost as a Rorschach inkblot personality test. To many the process appeared to be little more than an "incumbency protection plan."[5] As one legislator complained, "What happened to drawing lines for the people of the state rather than ourselves?"[6] During the entire decade between 2001 and 2010, only 1 of the 173 seats (120 in the state legislature and 53 in Congress) changed party hands.

In 2008, Governor Arnold Schwarzenegger joined with Common Cause, the League of Women Voters, and other reform groups to craft **Proposition 11, the Voters FIRST Initiative**. The ballot proposal placed redistricting in the hands of a fourteen-member independent commission composed of five Democrats, five Republicans, and four members not affiliated with either major party. Similar proposals had been defeated by the voters on seven previous occasions. This time, the voters approved the measure.

As of January 1, 2010, California's population was estimated at 38,600,000. So, during 2011, the state's new **Citizens Redistricting Commission** realigned legislative districts to be equal in size once again—482,500 for each assembly district and 965,000 in each senate district. Unlike the legislature's previous efforts, however, the Commission considered community geography and neighborhood compositions over political advantages associated with incumbency. Figures 5.1 and 5.2 show the same area of Southern California after the legislature's redistricting in 2001 and after the commission's work in 2011. Most new districts are much more compact than their predecessors.

With a new redistricting system in place, it remains to be seen whether the legislature will become less partisan and more effective. Table 5.1 displays the partisan breakdown of the legislature since 1985.

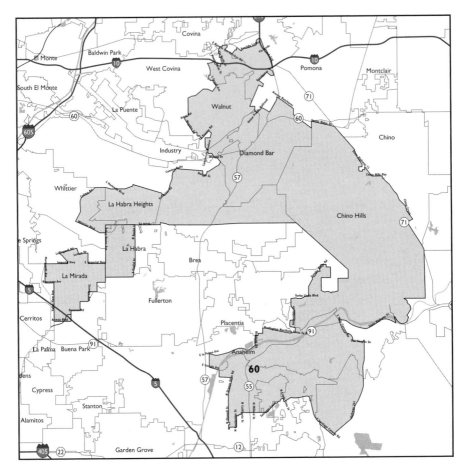

FIGURE 5.1 Map of Assembly District 60 after 2001 redistricting.

Term Limits

For some time, the public has been critical of the legislature's inability to solve thorny issues and pass on-time budgets. In 1990, the voters passed **Proposition 140**, an initiative that limited elected executive branch officers and state senators to two 4-year terms and assembly members to three 2-year terms, while reducing the legislature's operating budget (and thus its staff) by 38 percent.

Term-limits advocates envisioned a "turnstile" type of legislature, with members in office for relatively short periods. The system was designed to guarantee new faces, reduce the influence of money, and prevent incumbents from becoming entrenched in excess. Of the fifteen states currently with term limits, California has one of the most severe conditions in the nation. Unlike most other states with term limits, once state legislators in California complete their terms of service, they may never run for the legislature again.

Some objectives associated with **term limits** have been met, while others show no sign of coming to pass. New faces have certainly appeared—particularly women and minorities in much larger numbers than in the past—but in many

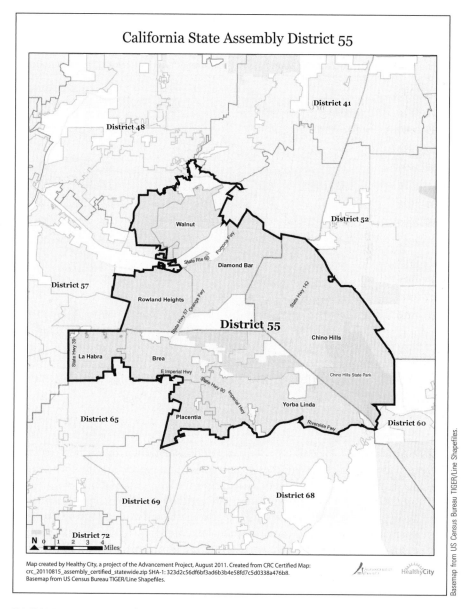

FIGURE 5.2 Map of Assembly District 55 after 2011 redistricting.

cases legislators have simply jumped from one house to the other. Nevertheless, those from relatively affluent backgrounds continue to be disproportionately elected to the legislature. In this sense, little has changed.

There also have been increasing instances of political cannibalism. Some **termed-out** assembly members have challenged senators from their own political party who are eligible to serve another term. In other cases, senators who have time left in the assembly have attempted to return to that house. In other instances still, termed-out legislators have returned home to run for county

T A B L E 5.1 Political Parties in the State Legislature, 1985–2014

Legislative Session	Senate			Assembly	
	Democrats	Republicans	Independents	Democrats	Republicans
1985–1986	25	15		47	33
1987–1988	24	15	1	44	36
1989–1990	24	15	1	47	33
1991–1992	27	12	2	47	33
1993–1994	23	15	2	49	31
1995–1996	21	17	2	39	41
1997–1998	22	17	1	42	38
1999–2000	25	15		48	32
2001–2002	26	14		50	30
2003–2004	25	15		48	32
2005–2006	25	15		48	32
2007–2008	25	15		48	32
2009–2010	25	15		50	30
2011–2012	25	13		52	28
2013–2014	29	11		55	25

SOURCE: California Secretary of State.

supervisor. The term-limits concept in California has spawned the state's version of "musical chairs."

Meanwhile, the overall costs of campaigning continue to set new records. Research also reveals that another significant impact of term limits has been a considerable decline in the quality of legislation since its adoption.[7]

Another criticism of term limits centers on the loss of legislative knowledge because of the rapid turnover. Because legislators have little opportunity to gain expertise, they tend to rely more on the governor and lobbyists,[8] the former because of policy experts who work as aids in the governor's office, and the latter because of the permanence of the lobbyists in the state capital. Legislators may be termed out, but lobbyists are not.

As a result of term limits, leadership positions in the legislature no longer carry the clout that once made that branch an effective counterweight to the executive branch. Current Assembly Speaker John Perez was elected to the assembly's highest post in 2010 with only a year of experience under his belt. Clearly, problems can develop with erratic leadership changes and inexperienced leaders.

Some of the leadership problems may have been addressed with the passage of **Proposition 28** in 2012. Effective 2014, legislators may serve all of their time in one house or the other, but with a limit of twelve years instead of fourteen. Proponents of this proposition believe that the ability to stay in one house for a longer time will allow legislators to develop more expertise.

Nationwide, the term limits movement seems to be abating. Four states with term limits have rejected the concept since 1999—Mississippi, Idaho, Oregon, and Utah. But in California, the voters continue to favor term limits. A public opinion poll in 2012 found that a resounding 62 percent of Californians supported the constraint, compared with only 12 percent who rejected it.[9]

New Rules, New Players

Redisricting, the change from part-time to full-time legislators, and term limits transformed the legislature, albeit unevenly. To be sure, the new framework attracted better-educated and more professional individuals and also made election to office more feasible for women and minorities. Thus, in 2013, the assembly included 21 women, 15 Latinos, 7 African Americans, 7 Asian Americans, and 5 openly gay members; the senate included 9 women, 8 Latinos, 3 African Americans, 2 Asian Americans, and 2 openly gay members (see Figure 5.3).

Despite greater diversity, the legislature has narrowed in terms of vocational backgrounds. During the 1980s, legislative aspirants from the business world were flanked by large numbers of lawyers, local activists, educators, and former legislative aides. But increasingly, the "business candidate" has emerged as the dominant category of self-description. During the 1990s, about half of all legislative candidates on the ballot listed some form of business as their occupation. Beginning in the late 1990s, large numbers of people from city- and county-elected posts also took seats in the legislature.[10] These patterns continue today.[11]

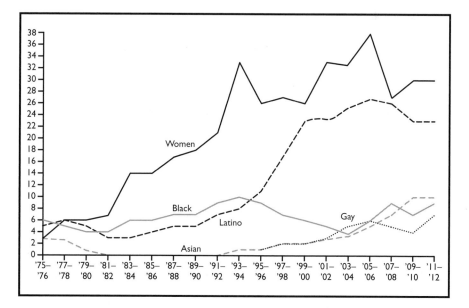

FIGURE 5.3 Women and Minorities in the California Legislature.

LEADERS AND STAFF MEMBERS

Although the two houses share lawmaking responsibilities, they function differently. Because the assembly is larger, it is more hierarchical in organization. The **speaker of the assembly** is clearly in charge of that body and wields considerable power. The speaker controls the flow of legislation, designation of committee chairs and assignments, and distribution of vast campaign funds to the members of his or her political party. The number of standing, or topical, committees varies each term with the speaker's term in office. For example, there were thirty such committees in the assembly during 2011–2012, the same as in the previous session. Some committees are far more important than others, so the speaker's friendship is of great value to a legislator. The speaker also may carry favor with the governor, especially if the two work well together.

By tradition, the party with a majority in the assembly chooses the speaker in a closed meeting, or caucus. A vote is then taken by the full assembly, with the choice already known to all. The minority party selects its leader in a similar fashion. Majority and minority floor leaders, as well as their whips (assistants), provide further support for the legislative officers. With solid majorities for most of the past half-century, the Democrats have controlled the speakership for all but four years during the period.

Before the term-limits era, speakers often held their posts for ten years or more. However, these days the tenures of speakers have been limited to between one and three years. The current speaker, John Perez, may stretch that life span a bit. He was elected to his post in 2009 and may serve through 2014, assuming he is reelected. His successor may fare even better in the post-Proposition 29 era if he or she elects to serve all or most of his or her twelve years in the assembly.

Prior to the court-ordered redistricting in 1966, the senate emphasized collegiality and cooperation over strong leadership, strict rules, and tight organization. But since then, the senate has been almost as partisan as the assembly. The most powerful member is the **president pro tem**, who, like the speaker, is elected by the majority party after each general election. The minority party also elects its leader at that time. The key to senate power lies with the five-member **Rules Committee**, which is chaired by the president pro tem and controls all other committee assignments and the flow of legislation. In 2011–2012 the senate had twenty-three standing committees, the same number as the previous session.

When Democrat John Burton presided as the pro tem, he used the office to raise and dispense large sums of money to grateful fellow Democrats. Burton was president pro tem for six years (1998–2004). More significantly, he had been an assembly member for nearly twenty years, mostly before the term limits era. Because of his experience, Burton became the legislature's lightning rod against Governor Arnold Schwarzenegger. Many observers viewed him as the legislature's most formidable leader, despite the assembly speaker's traditionally dominant role.

The current president pro tem, Democrat Darrell Steinberg, was elected to the position in 2008. He will not be termed out until 2014. Like most others in leadership positions, Steinberg assumed his post with relatively little senate experience, but his previous six years in the state assembly gave him a level of knowledge and influence exceeding that of his assembly counterpart, John Perez.

Although Democrats hold leadership positions in both houses, in recent years they have had trouble dealing with one another. Some of this difficulty may be due to the differing leadership styles of Senate President Pro Tem Steinberg and Assembly Speaker Perez. Steinberg has a record of crossing party lines to forge necessary, if distasteful, compromises. Perez has a reputation for being unwilling to part with core values.[12] Their internal gridlock has taken considerable pressure off the minority Republicans, who have watched internal struggles within the majority party with some glee. Nowhere has this been more evident than in the struggle to balance annual state budgets facing huge deficits. As the legislature grappled with its responsibilities in 2010, interest groups loyal to both sides actually began letter-writing campaigns and purchased television ads—all of which points to the lack of cohesion within the political parties.[13]

STAFFING THE PROFESSIONAL LEGISLATURE

The evolution of the legislature into a full-time body was accompanied by a major expansion of its support staff. These days about 2,200 staff assistants (commonly called "staffers") work for the members and committees—a far cry from the 485 employed by the last part-time legislature in 1966. Those in the capital usually concentrate on pending legislation and research, whereas staffers in the legislators' home district offices spend much of their time responding to constituents' problems.

Legislators spend much of their time in committees, the heart of the legislative process. Most committees cover specialized policy areas such as education or natural resources. A few, such as the senate and assembly rules committees, deal with procedures and internal organization. Each committee employs staff consultants who are experts on the committee's subject area and who are politically astute individuals in general—important attributes because they serve at the pleasure of the committee chair. Besides the traditional or standing committees, staffers assist more than sixty select committees that address narrow issues and nine joint committees that coordinate two-house policy efforts.

Another staff group is even more political. Employed by the Democratic and Republican caucuses in the senate and assembly, these assistants are supposed to deal with possible legislation. However, their real activities usually center on advancing the interests of their political party.

In addition to personal, committee, and leadership staffers, legislators have created neutral support agencies. With a staff of fifty-six, the **legislative analyst** (a position created in 1941) provides fiscal expertise, reviewing the annual budget and assessing programs that affect the state's coffers. The **legislative counsel** (created in 1913) employs about eighty attorneys to draft bills for legislators and determine their potential impact on existing legislation. The **state auditor** (created in 1955) assists the legislature by periodically reviewing and evaluating ongoing programs.

Historically, staffing has enhanced the legislature's professionalism. Yet some staffers, especially those who work for the legislative leaders, clearly spend more time on partisan politics than on legislation. Many have used their positions as apprenticeships to gain knowledge, skills, and contacts for their own campaign efforts or future employment as lobbyists. All this, critics point out, is funded by the taxpayers. Defenders of the system counter that this staffing arrangement helps compensate for weak party organizations and the information gaps associated with rapid legislative turnover.

HOW A BILL BECOMES A LAW

The legislature passes laws. It also proposes constitutional amendments, which are submitted for voter approval after they receive absolute two-thirds majority votes in both houses (the votes of two-thirds of the full membership—that is, twenty-seven votes in the senate and fifty-four in the assembly). The same absolute two-thirds majority votes are required for the legislature to offer bond measures—money borrowed for long-term, expensive state projects. Proposed constitutional amendments and bond measures must then obtain majority votes at the next election before becoming law.

Most of the legislature's energy, however, is spent on lawmaking. Absolute majorities—twenty-one votes in the senate and forty-one votes in the assembly—are required to pass the annual budget and basic laws intended to take effect the following January, but absolute two-thirds votes in both houses are required for urgency measures (those that become law immediately upon the governor's signature), and overrides of the governor's veto. The process, however, is far from simple.

The Formal Process

The legislative process begins when the assembly member or senator sponsoring a bill gives the clerk of the chamber a copy, which is recorded and numbered (see Figure 5.4). The process is known as moving the bill "across the desk" (of the receiving clerk), signifying that the proposed measure is now officially under consideration. The bill then undergoes three readings and several hearings before it is sent to the other house, where the process is repeated. The first reading simply acknowledges the bill's submission.

Depending upon the house of origin, either the senate Rules Committee or the assembly Rules Committee decides on the route of the bill. The chairs of these important committees can affect a bill's fate by sending it to "friendly" or "hostile" committees and by assigning it a favorable or unfavorable route. Typically, a bill is assigned to two or three committees for careful scrutiny by members who are experts in that bill's subject area. More than half of all bills die in committee, either through a formal vote or because the chair decides not to call for a vote.

Typically, between five thousand and six thousand bills are introduced during each two-year session, with assembly members limited to fifty proposals and senators limited to sixty-five. Given such volume, the **legislative committees** are essential to getting laws passed. They hold hearings, debate, and may eventually vote on each bill delegated to them. Most committees deal in narrow areas, but a few—such as the senate Budget and Fiscal Review Committee and the assembly Committee on Appropriations—focus on the collection and distribution of funds and thus enjoy clout that goes beyond any one policy area.

At the conclusion of its hearings, a committee can kill a bill, release it without recommendation, or approve it with a "do pass" proposal. It may also recommend approval contingent on certain changes or amendments, which can be substantial or minor and technical. Only when a bill receives a positive recommendation from all of the committees to which it was assigned is it likely to get a second reading by the full legislative body. At this stage, the house considers additional amendments. After all proposed revisions have been discussed, the bill is printed in its final form and presented to the full house for a third reading. After further debate on the entire bill, a vote is taken.

Sometimes, the bill changes so dramatically that the original author abandons sponsorship in disgust; the bill then dies unless another legislator assumes sponsorship. On other occasions, a bill is introduced about a topic of little significance or with little more than a number. Then, later in the term, when the deadline for introductions has passed, the author may strip the bill of its original language and offer replacement language to deal with a pressing topic new to the legislative agenda. This strategy, known as **gut-and-amend**, isn't pretty but gives a legislator flexibility he or she would not have otherwise. It also circumvents the normal legislative process of committee hearings and due deliberation, sometimes to the chagrin of some lobbyists and interest groups.

If a bill is approved by the members of one house, it goes to the other house, where the process starts anew. Again, the bill may die anywhere along the perilous legislative path. If the two houses pass different versions of the same bill, the versions must be reconciled by a **conference committee**. Senate members are appointed by the Rules Committee; assembly members are chosen by the speaker, yet another sign of the power that comes with that position. If the conference committee agrees on a single version and if both houses approve it by the required margins, the bill goes to the governor for his or her approval. Otherwise, the proposed legislation is dead.

Usually, a bill becomes law if the governor signs it or takes no action within twelve days. However, if it is passed immediately before a session's end, the governor has thirty days to act. If the governor vetoes a bill, an absolute two-thirds majority must be attained in both houses for it to become law. Attaining such a lopsided vote is next to impossible, so vetoed bills generally fall by the wayside.

The Informal Process

Politics permeates the formal, "textbook" process by which a bill becomes law. This means that every piece of legislation is considered not only on its merits but also on the basis of a variety of factors, including political support, interest group pressure, public opinion, and personal power.

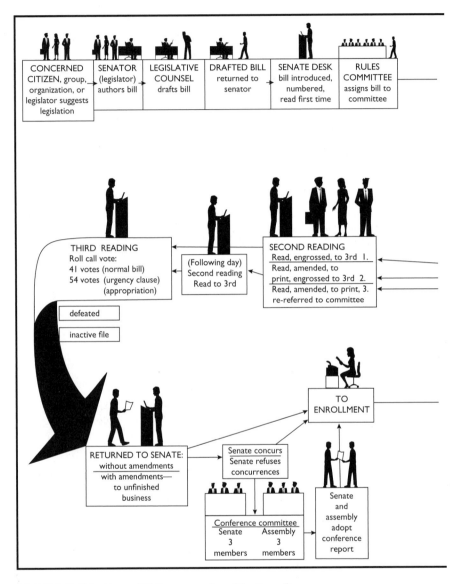

FIGURE 5.4 How a Bill Becomes a Law (Continued).

Members of the majority party chair most, if not all, of the committees in any given year. With Democrats in control for most of the last five decades, they have reaped the benefits of the committee chairs (extra staff, procedural advantages, and so forth), secured the best committee assignments, and been assigned the best offices. Likewise, when assembly Republicans briefly held a bare majority in 1996, they assumed control of twenty-five of the twenty-six committees, and the benefits were reversed.

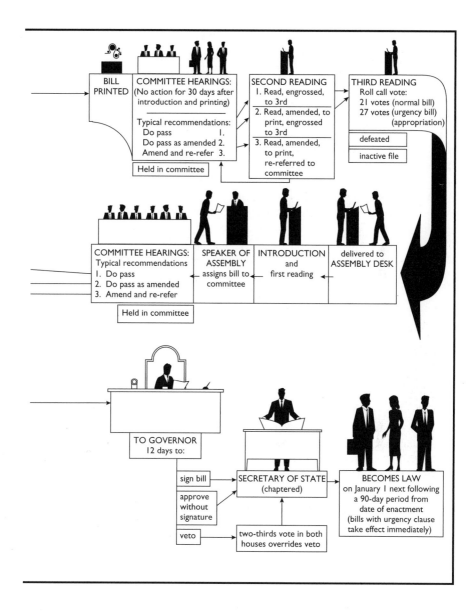

Political support within the legislature is essential to numerous decisions. So many bills flow through the process that members often vote on measures they haven't even read, relying on staff, committee, or leadership recommendations. Sometimes, a bill's fate rests with key legislative leaders, who can use their positions to stifle or speed up a proposal at various points in the legislative process. In the assembly, the speaker may actually appoint extra members to a committee temporarily to move a bill along. Outcomes are also affected by **logrolling**, a give-and-take bargaining process where legislators agree to support each other's bills. More often than not, legislators give away their votes on matters of little concern to them in hopes of mollifying opponents or pleasing powerful leaders. And on occasion, some members of the assembly have been known to cast the votes of other members by clicking their electronic devices. This illegal activity, called **ghost voting**,[14] can't take place in the senate, where members cast votes by a show of hands.

Public opinion also affects legislation, sometimes dramatically. Recent statutes on children's safety and health, cellphone use while driving, higher education opportunities for illegal immigrants, environmental quality, and homeowners' rights have been enacted in direct response to public concern.

As noted in Chapter 4, pressure from interest groups permeates the legislative process. The relationship between the private and public policy arenas has only intensified with the growth of a full-time, year-round legislature. The combined cost of legislative campaigns has soared from $7 million in 1966 to $101 million in 2010. With an average of just over $1 million per legislative seat, California's legislative elections are the most expensive state contests in the nation.[15] And given the millions of dollars spent by independent expenditure committees that were not tied officially to any candidate, the total spent on legislative campaigns in the state in all likelihood exceeded $150 million.

OTHER FACTORS

Personal power within the legislature remains a component of the political process, especially in cases of conflict. One such example occurred in 2008, when then senate president pro tem Don Perata and the Democratic majority of the senate Rules Committee blocked four Schwarzenegger nominees to the twelve-member California Parole Board. For months, Perata had complained about California's low parole rate, implying that the problem rested with the parole board. This action sent a clear message to both the board and the governor.[16]

Sometimes the mere threat of an initiative spurs legislative action. In 2012, medical marijuana advocates abandoned an initiative effort for statewide regulation when Assemblyman Tom Ammiano introduced a bill with many of the same objectives. Ammiano secured passage from the assembly but then had to withdraw the proposal after senate resistance. Conversely, the legislature's work on climate change was nearly undone in November 2010 by a business-sponsored initiative to delay implementation of AB 32. On this occasion, the voters elected to let the controversial law remain in place.

UNFINISHED BUSINESS

Today's legislature faces myriad issues, ranging from a poorly working public education system to a deteriorating infrastructure. Faced with revolving participants, the legislature operates with little stability and less tradition. Term limits, decimated state budgets (see Chapter 8), and recession for most of the last decade have added to the woes of this policymaking body. Until 2011, the absolute two-thirds vote requirement for the annual budget often delayed badly needed services for months at the beginning of each fiscal year. In 2010, the voters attempted to ease budget gridlock by passing **Proposition 25**, a ballot measure which reduced the required budget vote to a simple majority. And in 2012, Democrats won absolute two-thirds majorities in both houses, allowing them to pass controversial policies–including tax increases–without Republican obstruction. Whether this success hails a new era of party unity remains to be seen.

With all these pressures, legislators often seem to react to problems rather than to anticipate or solve them. As a consequence, public policies are made increasingly by initiative, the governor, or the courts. Nevertheless, the legislature continues to grapple with the leading issues of the day, and at least sometimes, lawmakers manage to overcome assorted obstacles in a fractured political environment to enact policies of substance.

NOTES

1. *Californians and Their Government*, Public Policy Institute of California Statewide Survey (San Francisco: PPIC, May 2012).

2. In general, the plan provided one senator per county. In a few cases, two low-populated counties shared a senator, and in one case, three low-populated counties—Alpine, Inyo, and Mono—shared a senator.

3. Legislators receive monthly allowances for cars (including gasoline and maintenance); life, health, dental, vision, and disability insurance; and a daily housing allowance when they are in session in Sacramento. On average these benefits amount to about $30,000 annually, almost all of which is nontaxable.

4. The other full-time legislatures are Alaska, Florida, Massachusetts, Michigan, New Jersey, New York, Ohio, Pennsylvania, and Wisconsin.

5. "Plan to Redraw Districts Passes," *Los Angeles Times*, September 14, 2001, p. B8.

6. *Ibid.*

7. Rene Bukovichik Van Vechten, "Taking the Politics Out of Politics? State Legislative Politics and Institutional Reform in Twentieth Century California" (Ph.D. diss., University of California, Irvine 2002), 203–213, p. 21.

8. "Report Chronicles Downside of Term Limits," Stateline.org, August 16, 2006, www.stateline.org/live/details/story?contentId=134247.

9. "Drop in Support for Cigarette Tax, Most Support Term Limits Change,"Public Policy Institute of California (San Francisco: PPIC, May 23, 2012).

10. Kathleen Les, "Mr. Mayor Goes to the Capitol," *California Journal* 30, no. 10 (October 1999): 36–38.

11. See Bruce E. Cain and That Kousser, *Adapting to Term Limits: Recent Experiences and New Directions* (San Francisco: Public Policy Institute of California, 2004), p. 15.

12. "Choosing Sides in State Budget Fiasco," *Los Angeles Times*, June 26, 2010, pp. A1, A14.

13. *Ibid.*

14. See "Ghost Voting: A Long History," *San Francisco Chronicle*, June 10, 2008, pp. A1, A16.

15. Institute for State Government and Politics, http://maplight.org/california/contributions.

16. "Dems Reject Two of Schwarzenegger's Parole Appointees," *Sacramento Bee*, June 26, 2008, p. A3.

LEARN MORE ON THE WEB

California State Assembly:
www.assembly.ca.gov

California State Senate:
www.senate.ca.gov

Campaign finance:
www.followthemoney.org

Daily politics and policy-related news:
www.rtumble.com

Legislative Analyst's Office:
www.lao.ca.gov

Legislative histories and bill analyses:
www.leginfo.ca.gov/bilinfo.html

National Conference of State Legislatures:
www.ncsl.org

Search for your legislator:
www.legislature.ca.gov/legislators_and_districts/districts/districts.html

Watch or listen to the legislature in session:
www.legislature.ca.gov/the_state_legislature/calendar_and_schedules
/audio_tv.html

LEARN MORE AT THE LIBRARY

Bill Boyarsky. *Big Daddy: Jesse Unruh and the Art of Power Politics*. Berkeley: University of California Press, 2008.

Willie L. Brown, Jr., and P. J. Corkery. *Basic Brown: My Life and Our Times*. New York: Simon & Schuster, 2008.

Gerald C. Lubenow, ed. *Governing California*, 2d ed. Berkeley, Calif.: Institute of Governmental Studies Press, 2006.

Gary F. Moncrief, Peverill Squire, and Malcolm Jewel. *Who Runs for the Legislature?* Upper Saddle River, N.J.: Prentice Hall, 2001.

Peter Schrag. *California: America's High Stakes* Experiment. Berkeley: University of California Press, 2006.

GET INVOLVED

Contact your state senator or assembly member to volunteer or apply for an internship in his or her district office. To find your representatives, go to: www.legislature.ca.gov/legislators_and_districts/districts/districts.html

6

✳

California Law: Politics and the Courts

CHAPTER CONTENTS

Courts are very much a part of the political process. Judges and politicians have always known this, but the public has been slower to understand the political nature of the judiciary. When governors—or presidents—make controversial appointments to the courts, however, judicial politics becomes a very public matter. Court decisions overturning popular initiatives have also made judicial politics apparent.

What makes the courts political? It's not just controversial judicial decisions or even the involvement of party politicians. Courts are political because their judgments are choices between public policy alternatives. When judges consider cases, they evaluate the issues before them both in terms of existing legislation and in the context of the U.S. and California constitutions. Rulings based on differing judicial interpretations of these documents help some people and hurt others. This is why the courts, like members of the executive and legislative branches, are subject to the attentions and pressures of California's competing interests, and this is why the courts are political.

THE CALIFORNIA COURT SYSTEM

The California court system is the largest in the nation, with more than two thousand judicial officers and twenty-one thousand court employees. The three levels within the system are linked, but each has its own responsibilities. Most cases begin and end at the lowest level. Only a few move up the state's judicial ladder through the appeals process (see Figure 6.1), and even fewer end up in the U.S. Supreme Court.

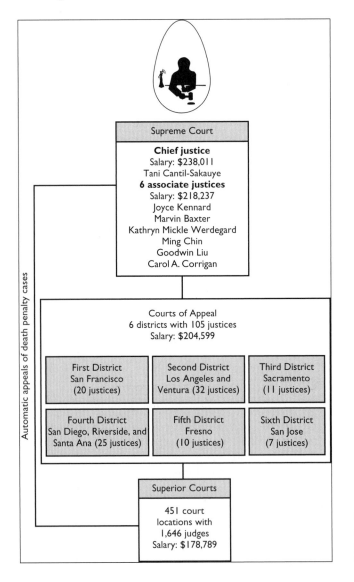

FIGURE 6.1 The California Court System.

SOURCE: California Judicial Council.

The Judicial Ladder

The vast majority of cases begin and end in trial courts, the bottom rung of the judicial ladder. In California, **superior courts** in each county are the trial courts, handling misdemeanor cases (minor crimes, including most traffic offenses), felonies (serious crimes subject to sentences of one year or more in state prison), civil suits (noncriminal disputes), divorces, and juvenile cases. Superior courts also operate small claims courts, where individuals can take cases with damage claims up to $10,000 before a judge without attorneys—sort of like television's *Judge Judy*.

Losers in trial courts may ask the court on the next rung of the judicial ladder to review the decision. Most cases aren't appealed, but when major crimes and penalties or big money are involved, the losers in the cases sometimes request a review by one of California's six district **courts of appeal**. As appellate bodies, these courts do not hold trials like the ones we see on television. Lawyers make arguments and submit briefs to panels of three justices, who try to determine whether the original trial was conducted fairly. These justices consider only possible legal errors, not the verdict in the case. If they find errors, they can send the case back for another trial or even dismiss the charges.

Ultimately, parties to the cases may petition for review by the seven-member state **supreme court**, the top of California's judicial ladder. Few cases reach this level because most are resolved in the lower courts and the high court declines most of the petitions. When the California Supreme Court hears a case, its decision is final unless issues of federal law or the U.S. Constitution arise; the U.S. Court may consider such cases.

If a higher court refuses an appeal, the lower court's decision stands. Even when a case is accepted, the justices of the higher court have agreed only to consider the issues. They may or may not overturn the decision of the lower court.

Judicial Election and Selection

Although the tiered structure of the California courts is similar to that of the federal courts, the selection of judges is not. Federal judges and members of the U.S. Supreme Court are appointed by the president subject to confirmation by the U.S. Senate. Once appointed, they serve for life. California judges and justices, however, gain office through a more complicated process and regularly face the voters. This periodic scrutiny by the public, the media, and interest groups helps keep judges and their decisions in the news.

Formal qualifications to become a judge are few: candidates must have been admitted to practice law in California for at least ten years. Technically, superior court judges are elected, but most actually gain office through appointment by the governor when a sitting judge dies, retires, or is promoted between elections, or sometimes when the legislature creates new judgeships. A governor who is elected to two terms of office may appoint as many as half of the state's sitting judges, significantly affecting judicial practices. Governors generally appoint judges who are members of their own political parties, although Republican Governor Arnold Schwarzenegger was more willing than any of his predecessors to appoint judges who were not members of his own political party. Prior service as a district attorney (prosecutor) has been common for successful appointees—a fact leading to complaints that judges are biased against defendants and defense attorneys. Governor Jerry Brown, however, has appointed several judges who have had experience as defense attorneys.

Appointed judges must run for office when their terms expire, but running as incumbents—often unopposed—they almost always win. Superior court judges can also gain office simply by declaring their candidacy for a specific judicial office—usually when there is a vacancy—and then running. If no candidate wins a majority in the primary election, the two candidates with the most votes face each other in a **runoff election** in November. Superior court judges serve six-year terms and then may run for reelection, usually without opposition. Judges have no term limits.

Appointments and the Higher Courts

Unlike lower court judges, members of the district courts of appeal and the state supreme court attain office only by gubernatorial appointment. The governor's possible nominees are first screened by the state's legal community through its Commission on Judicial Nominees Evaluation. Then the nominees must be approved by the **Commission on Judicial Appointments**, consisting of the attorney general, the chief justice of the state supreme court, and the senior presiding justice of the courts of appeal. The commission may reject a nominee, but it has done so only twice since its creation in 1934.

Once approved by the Commission on Judicial Appointments, the new justices take office, but they must go before the voters at the next gubernatorial election. No opponents or political party labels appear on the ballot; the voters simply check yes or no on the retention of the justices in question. If approved, they serve the remainder of the twelve-year term of the person they have replaced, at which time they can seek voter confirmation for a standard twelve-year term and additional terms after that.

Eleven other states select their supreme court justices in a similar fashion, but twenty-six rely solely on elections. The governor or legislature appoints justices in the remaining states.

Firing Judges

Almost all judges easily win election and reelection, mostly without opposition. Those who designed the system probably intended it to be this way. They wanted to distance judges somewhat from politics and to ensure their independence by giving them relatively long terms, thus also ensuring relatively consistent interpretation of the law. Avoiding costly election campaigns that depend on financial contributors also promotes independence. The framers of the U.S. Constitution put such a high value on judicial continuity and independence that they provided for selection by appointment rather than by election and allowed judges to serve for life. For most of California's history, these values also seemed well entrenched in the political culture, and the state's judges functioned without much criticism or interference. Nevertheless, California's constitution provides several mechanisms of judicial accountability. Judges can be removed through elections, but they can also be reprimanded or removed by the judicial system itself.

Incumbent justices of the California Supreme Court routinely win reelection without serious challenge. In the 1970s and 1980s, however, both high court justices and superior court judges faced challenges from critics of decisions that supported racial integration or were seen as lenient toward criminals. Some superior court judges were defeated and in 1986 Supreme Court Chief Justice Rose Bird and two other liberal justices appointed by Jerry Brown during his first term as governor were swept out of office—the only justices removed by the voters in California history. Since then, the anticourt fervor has subsided. Today, sitting judges are rarely challenged.

Judges also can be removed by the **Commission on Judicial Performance**, which investigates charges of misconduct or incompetence. Its members include three judges (appointed by the supreme court), two lawyers (appointed by the governor), and six public members (two each appointed by the governor, the senate Rules Committee, and the speaker of the assembly). Few investigations result in any action, but if the charges are confirmed, the commission may impose censure, removal from office, or forced retirement.

In 2011, the 1,168 complaints against judges were filed with the commission and 172 were investigated.[1] In the rare cases in which the commission finds a judge to be at fault, it issues a warning or reprimand. Even more rarely, the commission may remove a judge from the bench. In recent years, judges have been removed for lying about campaign funds, threatening a district attorney, inappropriate interventions in trials, and in one case, excessive delays and neglect of court orders. Actual removals from the bench are rare, however, because those whose conduct is questionable usually resign before the commission's investigation is completed.

THE COURTS AT WORK

In 2010–2011, 10,074,941 cases were filed in California's trial courts. Traffic infractions made up 58 percent of these cases. Felony and misdemeanor (criminal) cases numbered 1,571,494 (16 percent), and the balance were civil suits (such as liability or contract disputes) divorce, juvenile, or family law cases.[2]

California's constitution guarantees the right to a jury trial for both criminal and civil cases; if both parties agree, however, a judge alone hears the case. In jury trials, prospective jurors are drawn from lists of licensed drivers, voters, and property owners, but finding a twelve-member jury is often difficult. Many people avoid jury duty because it takes time away from work and pays only a few dollars a day. Homemakers and retired people are most readily available, but they alone cannot make up a balanced jury. Poor people and minorities tend to be underrepresented because they are less likely to be on the lists from which jurors are drawn and because some avoid participation in a system that they distrust.

The parties in civil cases provide their own lawyers, although legal aid societies sometimes help those who can't afford counsel. In criminal cases, the **district attorney**, an elected county official, carries out the prosecution. Defendants hire their own attorney or are provided with a court-appointed attorney if they cannot afford one. California's larger counties employ a **public defender** to provide such assistance. Well over half of all felony defendants require court-appointed help.

Most cases never go to trial, though. Over 97 percent of all criminal cases are settled out of court, mostly when the defendant pleads guilty and **plea bargaining** produces a pretrial agreement on a plea and a penalty. Plea bargaining reduces the heavy workload of the courts and guarantees some punishment or restitution, but it also allows those charged with a crime to serve shorter sentences than they might have received if convicted of all charges. Most civil suits are also settled without a trial because the parties to the cases reach an agreement to avoid the high costs and long delays of a trial. Only about 0.1 percent of all cases are tried before a jury (11,047 in 2009–2010); a judge alone hears the others that go to trial.[3]

It is important to note that the judicial system as a whole—including judges, prosecutors, public defenders, lawyers, and juries—does not reflect the diversity of California's people. About 72 percent of California's 175,617 active attorneys are non-Hispanic whites, even though minority group members make up 60 percent of the population. About one-third of the state's attorneys are women, however—a number that is quickly rising. Ethnic representation among California's judges is similar: 79 percent are male, and 72 percent are white.[4] These numbers lead critics to express concern about the fact that a predominantly white judicial system metes out justice to defendants who are, in the majority, nonwhite and that punishment is less severe for whites than for minorities convicted of the same crime.[5] African Americans, and to a lesser extent other minorities, perceive this situation and express deep mistrust of the system. Minority participation as attorneys and court officials has increased over time (Table 6.1 shows increasing diversity in judicial appointments), but considerable disparities remain.

Appeals

When a dispute arises over a trial proceeding or its outcome, the losing party may appeal to a higher court to review the case. Most appeals are refused, but the higher courts may agree to hear a case because of previous procedural problems (for instance, if the defendant was not read his or her rights) or because it raises untested legal issues. Appellate courts do not retry the case or review the facts in evidence; their job is to determine whether the original trial was fair and the law was applied appropriately. In addition to traditional appellate cases, the state supreme court automatically reviews all death penalty decisions. Although few in number (twenty-nine in 2009–2010), these cases take up a substantial

T A B L E 6.1 Judicial Appointments by California Governors, 1959–2011

	Male	Female	White	Black	Hispanic	Asian
Ronald Reagan (R), 1967–1975	97.4% (478)	2.6% (13)	93.1% (457)	2.6% (13)	3.3% (16)	1.0% (5)
Jerry Brown (D), 1975–1983	84.0 (691)	16.0 (132)	75.5 (621)	10.9 (90)	9.4 (77)	4.3 (35)
George Deukmejian (R), 1983–1991	84.8 (821)	15.2 (147)	87.7 (849)	3.6 (35)	5.0 (49)	3.6 (35)
Pete Wilson (R), 1991–1998	74.6 (517)	25.4 (176)	84.4 (585)	5.2 (36)	4.9 (34)	5.5 (38)
Gray Davis (D), 1999–2003	65.8 (237)	34.2 (123)	70.8 (255)	9.25 (33)	12.8 (46)	7.2 (26)
Arnold Schwarzenegger (R), 2003–2010	65.0 (370)	35.0 (199)	73.7 (419)	7.6 (43)	10.7 (61)	8.0 (46)
Jerry Brown (D), 2011–2012	62.9 (22)	37.1 (13)	51.5 (18)	17.1 (6)	20.0 (7)	11.4 (4)

SOURCE: Governor's Office.

amount of the supreme court's time. Neither the courts of appeal nor the state supreme court can initiate cases. No matter how eager they are to intervene in an issue, they have to wait for someone else to bring the case to them.

Every year, about 10,000 petitions are filed with the California Supreme Court, mostly requesting reviews of cases decided by the courts of appeal. Each year the members of the court, meeting "in conference," choose about two hundred petitions for consideration, a task that consumes an estimated 40 percent of the court's time. By refusing to hear a case, the court allows the preceding decision to stand. When the court grants a hearing, one of the justices (or a staff member) writes a "calendar memo" analyzing the case. Attorneys representing the two sides present written briefs and then oral arguments, during which they face rigorous questioning by the justices.

After hearing the oral arguments, the justices discuss the case "in conference" and vote in order of seniority; the chief justice casts the final, and sometimes decisive, vote. If the chief justice agrees with the majority, he or she can assign a justice to write the official court opinion; usually this is the same justice who wrote the initial calendar memo. A draft of the opinion then circulates among the justices, each of whom may concur, suggest changes, or write a dissenting opinion. Finally, after many months, the court's decision is made public. The court issued ninety-six opinions in 2009–2010—about 1 percent of all the petitions filed.

This time-consuming process allows plenty of room for politicking among the justices and depends on a high degree of cooperation and deferential behavior among them—what judges call **collegiality**—as a way of building consensus on issues under consideration. With seven independent minds on the court, ongoing negotiations are needed to reach a majority and a decision.

Managing the Courts

Besides leading the court through its decision making, the chief justice is responsible for managing the entire California court system and serves as chair of the **Judicial Council**, an appointed body of judges, attorneys, and legislators. The Judicial Council makes the rules for court procedures, collects data on the operations and workload of the courts, and oversees the Administrative Office of the Courts with 844 employees. The budget for the courts is set through the political process by the governor and the legislature and, like other state agencies, the courts have suffered budget cuts in recent years, despite an increased workload and complaints from the chief justice and other leaders of the judiciary. Reduced funding has resulted in political battles within the court system over whether to cut administrative or trial court costs.

THE HIGH COURT AS A POLITICAL BATTLEGROUND

The courts are especially important and powerful in California because of the nature of California government and politics. The state constitution has been amended more than five hundred times since it was written in 1879, making it both long and elaborately specific, with components addressing all sorts of matters, both major and mundane—and its density is constantly increased by initiatives. The length, detail, and continually changing complexity of California's constitution enhance the power of the state courts because they have the job of determining whether laws and public policy are consistent with the constitution. One scholar called the courts a "shadow government"[6] because of their importance in shaping public policy, but others view this as the courts' appropriate constitutional role.

The state supreme court is the ultimate interpreter of the state constitution (unless issues arise under the U.S. Constitution). The court's power makes it a center of political interest: governors strive to appoint justices who share their values and choose their appointees carefully. As governors have changed, so have the sorts of justices they appoint. And as its membership has changed, the California Supreme Court has moved across the spectrum from liberal to conservative.

Regardless of its collective political values, the court has not backed away from tackling controversial issues, including occasionally overturning decisions of the legislature or the people (as expressed in initiatives). This willingness is less because of interventionist attitudes on the part of the justices than because of a long, complex, and frequently amended constitution and poorly written laws and initiatives.

Governors, Voters, and the Courts

Long dominated by liberals, California's supreme court took a distinct turn toward the right in 1986, after the voters rejected the reelections of three liberal justices, including Rose Bird, the controversial chief justice at the time.

Appointed in 1977 by then-Governor Jerry Brown, Bird and her colleagues waded into controversy with unpopular rulings on busing for school desegregation and Proposition 13 (the popular property tax reduction initiative), as well as consistently reversing death sentences even as public concern about crime increased. When Bird and two other liberal justices were on the ballot in 1986, conservative Republican Governor George Deukmejian led a successful campaign to defeat them. With three new openings, Deukmejian transformed the court with conservative appointees, including a new chief justice.

Subsequent appointees have maintained the court's conservative majority. Today's court includes Marvin Baxter and Joyce Kennard (both Deukmejian appointees); Kathryn Werdegar and Ming Chin (appointed by Republican Governor Pete Wilson) and Carol A. Corrigan and Chief Justice Tani Cantil-Sakauye (both appointed by Governor Arnold Schwarzenegger). The newest member of the court—and its only Democrat—is Gordon Liu, appointed by Governor Jerry Brown in 2011. Minority members of the court include Cantil-Sakauye (who is Filipina), Liu and Chin (who are Chinese), and Kennard (who is Dutch-Indonesian). Four of the court's seven members are women. All of the current justices have won voter approval, with 65 to 76 percent voting for their retention. Cantil-Sakauye was confirmed for a twelve-year term by the voters in 2010 and Justice Liu will be up for confirmation in 2014.

With a majority of the justices appointed by Republican governors and solidly confirmed by the voters, California's supreme court today is moderately conservative and less controversial than in the past. The court's conservatism is reflected in its tendency to be pro-prosecution in criminal cases and pro-business in economic cases. The court also disappointed local governments seeking new taxes with rulings that rigidly applied a requirement for two-thirds voter approval, a strict interpretation of 1978's Proposition 13 (see Chapter 8) and when they upheld the right of the state to dissolve local redevelopment agencies (see Chapter 9).

Overall, the supreme court avoids **judicial activism** (making policy through court decisions rather than through the legislative or electoral process), but even the current conservative court sometimes asserts its independence, wading into political controversy and significantly affecting state politics. For example, it has followed the Bird court's precedent of approving state-funded abortions and the court rejected plans by the Governor Schwarzenegger and state legislature to solve their own budget problems by taking transportation and redevelopment funds from local governments. In 2011, the Republican-dominated court rejected an appeal by the state Republican Party to overturn the legislative districts by the voter-created Citizens Redistricting Commission (see Chapter 5), upholding the work of the commission.

Most controversially, the courts sometimes overrule decisions of the voters, as they did when they struck down portions of voter-approved initiatives that required tougher sentences for criminals because the proposals shifted discretion from judges to prosecutors. Probably the highest-profile and most controversial action taken by the California Supreme Court, however, was its 2008 ruling on same-sex marriage. When the city and county of San Francisco licensed such marriages in 2004, the supreme court ruled the marriages illegal on the basis of state law, as approved by the voters in 2002. But the constitutionality of that law was challenged in 2008, and on a four-to-three vote, the court ruled that "the California Constitution properly must be interpreted to guarantee this basic civil right to all Californians, whether gay or heterosexual, and to same-sex couples as well as to opposite-sex couples."[7] Opponents quickly qualified **Proposition 8**, an initiative constitutional amendment to restrict marriage to opposite-sex couples. Voters approved the measure, thus overruling the court. That initiative was subsequently challenged in court, but the California Supreme Court accepted it as a legitimate amendment to the state constitution. Then Chief Justice George wrote that the court's decision was not based on whether Proposition 8 "is wise or sound as a matter of policy," but rather "concerns the right of the people … to change or alter the state constitution itself.… Regardless of our views as individuals on this question of policy, we recognize as judges and as a court our responsibility to confine our consideration to a determination of the constitutional validity and legal effect of the measure in question."[8]

This decision did not put the issue to rest, however. The federal courts are sometimes drawn into battles over California initiatives, too. Since the 1990s, federal courts have overturned initiatives on campaign finance, open primary elections, and limits on public services for immigrants as violations of the U.S. Constitution, which trumps any state law or state constitution. In 2010, proponents of same-sex marriage took their case to a federal district court, arguing that Proposition 8 constituted a denial of equal rights under the U.S. Constitution. The judge in that case ruled in favor of the plaintiffs, thus overriding both the voters of the state of California and the state supreme court. The federal court ruling is being appealed, and the final decision will rest with the U.S. Supreme Court—or the voters of California when the issue comes back to them in yet another initiative.

Judicial rulings against voter-approved laws may appear undemocratic, but the courts are doing their duty by interpreting these controversial propositions not only for their content but also for their consistency with the California and U.S. constitutions. When the courts find an act of another branch of government or of the voters to be contrary to existing law or to the state or federal constitution, it is their responsibility to overturn that law, even if their decision is unpopular. "When we invalidate one of these initiatives," former chief justice George argued, "what we are doing is not thwarting the public's will. We are adhering to the ultimate expression of the popular will: the Constitution of the United States, or the Constitution of the State of California, which has been adopted by the people and which imposes limits on the initiative process and on lawmaking by legislatures and by the executive."[9]

As controversial as the California Supreme Court's decisions sometimes are, the court's influence goes well beyond this state. A study of court decisions throughout the country found that courts in other states followed precedents set in California more than precedents set in the courts of any other state.[10] This suggests that the California court is well within the mainstream of jurisprudence in the United States. It's also one reason why the court battle over same-sex marriages was so hard fought.

COURTS AND THE POLITICS OF CRIME

Crime topped the list of voter concerns in California and the nation during much of the 1980s and 1990s. Murder, rape, burglary, gang wars, and random violence seemed all too common. Republicans were elected governor at least partly because they were seen as law-and-order candidates.

Capital punishment was a key issue in the 1980s, when a liberal supreme court overturned the vast majority of the death penalty cases it reviewed. Since 1986, when the voters rejected these liberals, the supreme court has affirmed most death sentences. The issue has not gone away, however. Law-and-order advocates condemn the lengthy and costly delays that plague death penalty appeals—up to ten years for the state courts and another ten years for the federal courts—but experts say that much of the delay is caused by the inability of the courts to find legal counsel for the condemned or handle the workload. Meanwhile, forensic methods such as DNA testing have revealed wrongful convictions in death penalty cases and the federal courts have suspended executions in California due to concerns about the drugs used for lethal injections and the conditions of outdated prison facilities for executions.

Over seven hundred condemned murderers are on death row and none has been executed since 2006. The system has been called "broken" and "dysfunctional" and Chief Justice Cantil-Sakauye has said the death penalty is "not effective."[11] Arguing that capital punishment constitutes "cruel and unusual punishment" and that it actually costs more than life imprisonment, reformers put a proposition banning the death penalty on the 2012 ballot, but with polls showing continued strong voter support for capital punishment, the measure was defeated.

The law-and-order movement of the 1980s and 1990s also produced a series of propositions that strengthened penalties for many crimes, including the "three-strikes" initiative in 1994. Reflecting the view that liberal judges who were "soft on crime" were letting criminals off with light sentences, "**three strikes**" required anyone convicted of three felonies to serve a sentence of twenty-five years to life: "three strikes and you're out."

The three-strikes law quickly increased the state's prison population, as well as spending on prisons (see Chapter 8). With many of the state's worst criminals incarcerated for life, three-strikes prosecutions declined, and so did California's crime rate. Violent crime in California peaked in 1992 (two years before the three-strikes law) and has declined since then. In 2010 the number of violent crimes was lower than in 1979, even with 15 million more people living in the state.[12] Conservatives attribute this decline to tougher judges and penalties, but many experts argue that the declining crime rate was due to economic prosperity and demographics, with fewer people in the age group most commonly associated with criminal activity. Even in the recent recession, crime rates continue to decline. With crime less of a worry and concerns that the three-strikes law was too tough when the third strike was a minor crime, voters approved a 2012 ballot measure restricting third-strike penalties to serious, violent crimes.

Meanwhile, the prison population in California is huge, which means the cost of incarcerating all these men and women is also huge. But despite a massive

investment of tax funds, California's prisons are overcrowded and beset by violence and disease. A system built for 84,271 inmates housed 173,479 in 2006 (a
historic high).[13] Conditions in the prison health-care system were so bad that a
class action suit was brought to a federal court, which intervened on grounds that
these conditions constituted "cruel and unusual punishment" under the U.S.
Constitution. In 2005 a federal judge put the prison health system in the hands
of a court-appointed monitor. In 2009, seeing minimal progress, federal judges
ordered the state to come up with a plan to reduce the prison population. The
state of California appealed to the U.S. Supreme Court but in 2011, the court
ruled against the state and ordered a substantial reduction in prison population
within two years on grounds that overcrowding and health concerns violated the
U.S. Constitution. Governor Brown responded by transferring lesser, nonviolent
offenders from prisons to county jails. Designated "**realignment**," this system
reduced the prison population as well as the cost of incarceration, since jails are
cheaper to operate, but it also imposed new responsibilities and costs on local
governments (see Chapter 9).

CALIFORNIA LAW

Crime and other issues discussed in this chapter remind us that the courts play a
central role in the politics of our state. Controversies about judicial appointments
and decisions make the political nature of the courts apparent, especially when the
rulings of the court conflict with the will of the electorate as expressed in initiatives. Yet the courts can never be free of politics. They make policy and interpret
the law, and their judgments vary with the values of those who make them.

NOTES

1. State of California Commission on Judicial Performance, 2011 Annual Report,
   http://cjp.ca.gov (accessed August 15, 2012).
2. Judicial Council of California, *2011 Court Statistics Report*, www.courts.ca.gov
   (accessed August 17, 2012).
3. *Ibid.*
4. "Governor Brown Releases 2011 Judicial Appointment Data," Office of the
   Governor, March 1, 2012, http://gov.ca.gov/news.php?id=17437 (accessed
   August 16, 2012).
5. Elsa Y. Chen, "Cumulative Disadvantage and Racial and Ethnic Disparities in
   California Federal Sentencing," in *Racial and Ethnic Politics in California*, ed.
   Sandra Bass and Bruce M. Cain (Berkeley: Public Policy Press, Institute of
   Governmental Studies, University of California, 2008).
6. Charles Price, "Shadow Government," *California Journal*, October 1997, p. 38.
7. *In re Marriage Cases*, S147999.

8. *Strauss v. Horton*, S168047; *Tyler v. State of California*, S168066; and *City and County of San Francisco v. Horton*, S168078, www.courtinfo.ca.gov/courts/supreme.

9. Ronald George, "Promoting Judicial Independence," *Commonwealth*, February 2006, p. 10.

10. Jake Dear and Edward W. Jesson, "Followed Rates and Leading Cases, 1940–2005," *University of California, Davis, Law Review* 41 (April 2007): 683.

11. California Commission on the Fair Administration of Justice, "Fair Administration of the Death Penalty," June 30, 2008, www.ccfaj.org (accessed August 17, 2012) and 12/24/2011, "Top Judge Casts Doubt on Capital Punishment," *Los Angeles Times*, December 24, 2011.

12. "California Crime Rates, 1960–2010," www.disastercenter.com/crime/cacrime.htm (accessed August 17, 2012).

13. Department of Corrections, "Population Reports," www.cdcr.ca.gov (accessed August 17, 2012).

LEARN MORE ON THE WEB

California's court system:
www.courts.ca.gov

Justice Corps (service learning):
www.courts.ca.gov/programs-justicecorps.htm

For more on the courts:
www.judgepedia.org

State Bar of California:
www.calbar.org

Ratings of attorneys:
www.avvo.com

LEARN MORE AT THE LIBRARY

Rodney F. Kingsnorth, "Change How We Appoint Judges," in *Remaking California*, ed. R. Jeffrey Lustig (Berkeley: Heyday Books, 2010).

Preble Stolz, Gerald F. Uelmen, and Susan Rasky, "The California Supreme Court," in *Governing California*, 2d ed., edited by Gerald C. Lubenow. Berkeley: Berkeley Public Policy Press, Institute of Governmental Studies, University of California, 2006.

GET INVOLVED

You can learn about law and the courts through the Justice Corps, an Americorps service learning program with some compensation: www.courts.ca .gov/programs-justicecorps.htm.

7

✳

The Executive Branch: Coping with Fragmented Authority

CHAPTER CONTENTS

I f California's executive branch were composed solely of the governor, appointed department heads, and the civil service system, it would parallel the federal executive branch. But the state's executive branch also includes a lieutenant governor, an attorney general, a secretary of state, a controller, a treasurer, an insurance commissioner, a superintendent of public instruction, and a five-member Board of Equalization. All are elected at the same time and serve four-year terms. Unlike the president and vice president, though, who are elected on the same political party ticket, each of these officeholders runs independently. The result is a cluttered branch of state government with competing sources of power.

Endless schisms between officeholders in the executive branch contribute to the state's jurisdictional fragmentation. Occasionally, these executives clash over the use of authority, leading to political stalemate or conflicts in the courts, and most of all confusion among the electorate. Thus, the executive branch is anything but a unified body.

THE GOVERNOR: FIRST AMONG EQUALS

The **governor** is California's most powerful public official. He or she shapes the state budget, appoints key policymakers in the executive and judicial branches, and both responds to and shapes public opinion by taking positions on controversial issues. The governor also is the state's chief administrator; the unofficial leader of his or her political party; and liaison to other states, the U.S. government, and other nations. On occasion, the governor's powers extend even to international issues such as immigration or global warming.

The current governor of California, Democrat Edmund J. ("Jerry") Brown, Jr., was elected in 2010. Brown succeeded Arnold Schwarzenegger, who had been elected after the recall of Gray Davis from office (see Table 7.1). With an annual salary of $165,288, the office ranks tenth among the highest-paid chief executives of the fifty states. The pay was $212,179 as recently as 2009, but hard times have led the state Salary Compensation Commission to cut the governor's salary along with those of other elected state officials three years in a row. In fact, the governor's salary is well below the incomes earned by many other government employees in California, particularly in large cities and counties, as well as the heads of University of California and California State University campuses. Even among state employees, prison wardens, retirement program coordinators, and physicians earn considerably more than the governor.

T A B L E 7.1 California Governors and Their Parties, 1943–2015

Name	Party	Dates in Office
Earl Warren	Republican*	1943–1953
Goodwin J. Knight	Republican	1953–1959
Edmund G. Brown, Sr.	Democrat	1959–1967
Ronald Reagan	Republican	1967–1975
Jerry Brown	Democrat	1975–1983
George Deukmejian	Republican	1983–1991
Pete Wilson	Republican	1991–1999
Gray Davis	Democrat	1999–November 2003
Arnold Schwarzenegger	Republican	2003–2011
Jerry Brown	Democrat	2011–2015

*Warren cross-filed as both a Republican and a Democrat in 1946 and 1950.
SOURCE: California Secretary of State.

Jerry Brown's election to the governor's office is the latest example of California's bizarre politics. A political fixture in the state since his first election to the Los Angeles Community College District Board of Trustees in 1969 (that's not a typo!), Brown was elected governor in 1974 and 1978 after serving as the secretary of state. His father, Edmund G. (Pat) Brown also was elected governor in 1958 and 1962. Because his governorship occurred before California adopted term limits in 1990, Jerry Brown was eligible to run again. With his third term Brown is in rare company. Only Earl Warren was elected to three terms in the pre-term limit era.

Brown's election is significant in another way: he was outspent by a margin of more than 6-to-1, courtesy of opponent Meg Whitman's largely self-funded campaign in which the Republican donated $175 million to her ill-fated cause. Indeed, a key theme of Brown's campaign accused Whitman of trying to buy the governorship. Apparently there was no sale.

Formal Powers

Much of the governor's authority comes from formal powers written into the state's constitution and its laws. These responsibilities guide his or her relationships with the legislative and judicial branches, as well as with the other officeholders in the executive branch.

Submission of an Annual Budget.   No formal power is more important than the governor's budgetary responsibilities. The state constitution requires the governor to recommend a balanced budget to the legislature within the first ten days of each calendar year. The budget outlines the sources of state revenues and the recipients of state funds. Budget work is virtually a year-round task, consuming more of the governor's time than just about any other activity except emergencies such as earthquakes or fires. The governor is assisted in this effort by an appointed **director of finance**, who crafts the budget document after gathering data and funding requests from the dozens of departments and agencies within the state's bureaucracy. Initial preparations begin on July 1—the start of the fiscal year—and culminate with the governor's submission of a proposal to the legislature the following January (see Chapter 8). Officially, the process ends with the signing of the budget by the governor before the end of the fiscal year on June 30, so that the next year can begin with a budget in place.

Vetoes.   Under most circumstances, the governor has twelve days to act after the legislature passes a bill. On the hundreds of bills enacted by the legislature at a session's end, however, the governor has thirty days to act. Only a veto can keep a bill from becoming law. After the governor's time limit has passed, any unsigned or unvetoed bill becomes law the following January, unless the bill is an urgency measure, in which case it takes effect immediately upon signature. Governors use the **general veto**, which rejects a bill in its entirety. This exercise of power can be overturned only by an absolute two-thirds vote in each house, which rarely occurs.

The governor has special powers on spending bills passed by the legislature, many of which are associated with passage of the annual state budget. With spending bills, the governor cannot add money, but he or she can reduce or eliminate expenditures through use of the **item veto** before signing the budget into law. As with the general veto, an absolute two-thirds vote from each house of the legislature is necessary to overturn item vetoes. Because of that high threshold, legislators often attempt to head off vetoes by negotiating with the governor in advance.

Between 1982 and 2012, five successive governors exercised general and item vetoes without any repercussions from the legislature, and they did so with increasing frequency (see Table 7.2). More than any governor in history, Arnold Schwarzenegger turned the veto into a potent legislative weapon by rejecting more than one-fourth of the bills that reached his desk. The current governor, Jerry Brown, has used the veto more prudently. Ironically, the last time the legislature overturned a governor's veto was in 1979 when Jerry Brown was governor.

Special Session.   If the governor believes that the legislature has not addressed an important issue, he or she can take the dramatic step of calling a **special session**. At that time, the lawmakers must discuss only the specific business proposed by the governor. Special sessions often are called to respond to specific crises, as when Governor Schwarzenegger called on the legislature in 2006 to correct a prison system so overcrowded that a federal judge assumed oversight responsibilities. He also called special sessions on health-care reform, water policy, public education, and repeatedly on state budget deficits. Schwarzenegger called sixteen special sessions during his years in office—the most of any governor in state history—leading some to believe that he had diluted the significance of the concept.[1]

Executive Order.   On occasion, the governor can make policy by signing an **executive order**, an action that looks similar to legislation. Governors must

TABLE 7.2 Vetoes and Overrides, 1967–2012

Governor	Bills Vetoed (%)	Vetoes Overridden
Ronald Reagan (1967–1975)	7.3	1
Jerry Brown (1975–1983)	6.3	13
George Deukmejian (1983–1991)	15.1	0
Pete Wilson (1991–1999)	16.6	0
Gray Davis (1999–November 2003)	17.6	0
Arnold Schwarzenegger (November 2003–2011)	26.4	0
Jerry Brown (2011–2012)	13.1	0

SOURCE: Clerk, California State Senate.

exercise this power carefully because such moves often lead to lawsuits over the breadth of their powers. Shortly after taking office in 2011, Jerry Brown signed several orders designed to curb state spending in the face of the state's huge budget deficit. They included a state hiring freeze, drastic cutbacks on the purchase of state automobiles, and even the return of 48,000 cell phones used by state employees. Said Brown, "In the face of a multibillion-dollar budget deficit, a cellphone might not seem like a big expense, but spending $20 million, and perhaps far more than that, on cell phones can't be justified."[2]

Appointment Powers.   Before the Progressive reforms, California governors used patronage, or the "spoils" system, to hire friends and political allies. Today, 99 percent of all state employees are not appointed by the governor but rather are selected through a civil service system based on merit. Still, the governor fills about 2,500 key positions in the executive departments and cabinet agencies, except for the Departments of Justice and Education, whose heads are elected by the public. Together, these appointees direct the state bureaucracy (see Figure 7.1).

The state senate must approve most of the governor's appointees. Generally, senate confirmation is routine, but occasionally the governor's choice for a key post is rejected for reasons other than qualifications. In instances of an opening in the executive branch, both houses must weigh in with positive majorities. In early 2010, Governor Schwarzenegger nominated Republican State Senator Abel Maldonado to fill the lieutenant governor vacancy resulting from Lieutenant Governor John Garamendi's election to a vacated congressional seat. After several months of fits and starts, Maldonado was confirmed, only to lose in the November 2010 general election to Democrat Gavin Newsom.

The governor also appoints people to more than three hundred state boards and commissions. Membership on some boards—such as the Arts Council and the Commission on Aging, which have only advisory authority—is largely ceremonial and without pay. Other boards, however, such as the California Energy Commission (CEC), the Public Utilities Commission (PUC), the California Coastal Commission (CCC), and the California Air Resources Board (CARB) make important policies free from direct gubernatorial control. Nevertheless, the governor affects key "independent" boards through his or her appointments and manipulation of the budget.

Perhaps the most enduring of all gubernatorial appointments are judgeships. The governor fills both vacancies and new judgeships that are periodically created by the legislature. Most judges continue to serve long after those who appointed them have gone. However, the governor's power is checked here to a degree, too, by various judicial commissions and by the voters in future elections. During his tenure as governor, Arnold Schwarzenegger was much less partisan with his judicial appointments than his predecessors (see Chapter 6). Current Governor Jerry Brown has acknowledged the state's diversity by appointing high numbers of people of color and women to judicial posts.

In addition to the major areas of formal authority discussed earlier, the governor has a wide range of other formal powers. He or she is commander in chief

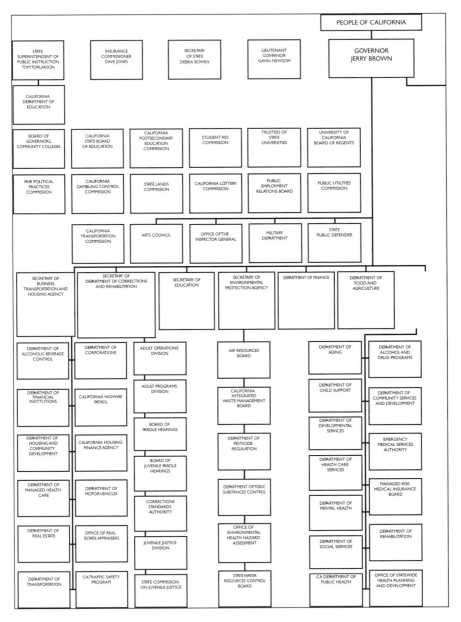

FIGURE 7.1 State Departments and Agencies.

of the California National Guard, which on occasion is sent to help manage local crises in the state on a short-term basis. The governor also has the power to grant pardons, reprieves, or sentence commutations, although such authority is rarely exercised. Finally, the governor is the ceremonial head of state for greeting dignitaries from other countries. Along with the other major functions, these powers keep the governor very active and in the public eye.

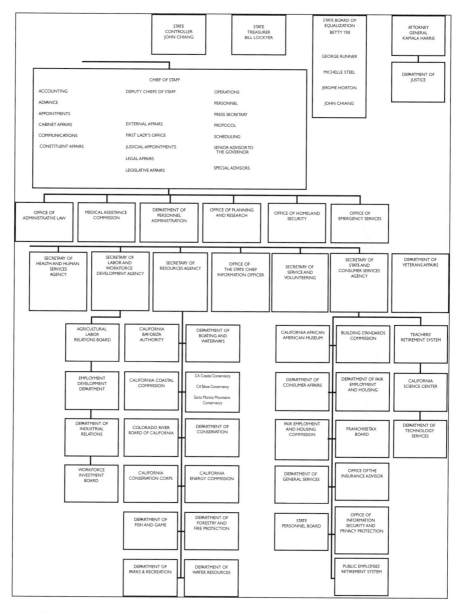

FIGURE 7.1 (Continued)

Informal Powers

Formal constraints on the governor can be offset to some extent by a power that is not written into the constitution at all, yet effective nonetheless: the governor's popularity. When the governor is in good stead with other legislators and/or the public, he or she is often able to overcome political opponents.

Historically, California's governors have used the prestige of their office to push their own agendas. Republican Governor Pete Wilson touted **Proposition 187**, an attempt to reduce government benefits to illegal immigrants that was ultimately rejected by the federal courts. In 1996 Wilson championed **Proposition 209**, titled the California Civil Rights Initiative, to eliminate affirmative action. And in 1998 he promoted **Proposition 227**, an initiative restricting bilingual education. These initiatives benefitted Wilson initially but have since hurt the Republican party's reputation with the state's increasingly diverse racial and ethnic diversity—a stigma that remains to this day.

Democratic Governor Gray Davis operated with a personality that left little room for disagreement. He attacked the other branches of state government, claiming that state legislators were supposed to implement his vision[3] and that judicial appointees should reflect his views.[4] His obsession with constant fund-raising from individuals and organizations in search of state business added to his image problems. When Davis was reelected in 2002, the state suffered a perfect storm with exorbitant energy costs, a lengthy recession, and huge budget shortfalls. As the state's condition worsened, the voters lost patience with Davis. In a July 2003 Field poll, 61 percent of the respondents blamed Davis for the state's problems.[5] Thus, as an unprecedented recall effort moved along during 2003, Davis first lost his public support and informal power, and soon after that, his job.[6]

Arnold Schwarzenegger used his informal power to circumvent the legislature whose members he called "girlie men" for not adopting his budgets.[7] Repeatedly, he cut deals directly with organizations and institutions from local governments to universities, prison guards, and Indian gaming interests. In 2010, Schwarzenegger negotiated pension reforms with several state employee unions that mandated higher employee contributions—something the legislature had not dared to even tackle.[8]

Schwarzenegger had mixed results with the voters. In March 2004 he successfully barnstormed the state for a ballot measure, described as a $15 billion "recovery" bond that temporarily balanced the state budget. But in 2005 Schwarzenegger suffered a stinging defeat, when voters rejected his ballot measures on teacher tenure, union campaign contributions, strict state budget controls, and legislative redistricting. His standing in public opinion polls plummeted from 64 percent to 35 percent in ten short months,[9] and he never fully recovered.

Still, Schwarzenegger used his personality even in defeat to reconnect with the public. Immediately after the 2005 election, he reflected, "I should have listened to my wife [prominent Democrat Maria Shriver], who said don't do this."[10] That self-effacing approach helped gain Schwarzenegger reelection in 2006. But his ballot box success was short-lived. In 2009, Schwarzenegger asked voter support for a series of five budget-related initiatives; all were rejected.

Schwarzenegger's vision often exceeded his ability to deliver. In successive years, he declared the "year" of political reform, which ended with the defeat of four Schwarzenegger-tailored ballot measures; the "year" of health-care reform, which fizzled in the legislature; and the "year" of education reform, which sputtered out after he cut public funding several years in a row to leave

California near the bottom of the fifty states in per capita spending. More times than not, Schwarzenegger's performance failed to match his bravado.

Jerry Brown has approached his current occupancy of the governorship much differently than his first go-around thirty-six years earlier. With his election in 2010 at the age of seventy-two, Brown became the oldest person to be elected to the position; coincidentally, when he was elected in 1974 at the age of thirty-six, he was the state's youngest in history, a record that stands to this day. During his first two terms, Brown had a contentious relationship with the legislature. He was nicknamed "Governor Moonbeam" for a variety of futuristic, and sometimes whimsical proposals thought by many to be couched in anything but reality.

That was then. Between stints in the governor's office, Brown was chair of the state Democratic party, served as mayor of Oakland, and elected state attorney general. And he married. The totality of these experiences and more helped facilitate the transformation of Jerry Brown.

In his first two years of the current term, Brown has shown a blend of patience and quiet urgency with the legislature about solving the state's issues. He has assiduously courted Democrats and Republicans, liberals and conservatives. His efforts notwithstanding, Brown has not been able to suture the differences within the legislature. As he recently lamented, "There's not a thread of common purpose" between the two sides.[11]

Still, Brown has persevered. He has battled with the legislature on the budget, going so far as to veto the entire document in 2011 before accepting a modified version (see Chapter 8 for budget issues). Elsewhere, in 2011 he convinced the legislature to pass his **"realignment"** plan to move nonviolent prisoners from state facilities to less expensive county jails. In 2012, he persuaded the legislature to spend most of a $10 billion bond on the first leg of the state's proposed high-speed rail system, despite skittish public opinion and uncertain future funds. In the same year, he helped narrow future state budget deficits by securing agreements from public employee unions on wage cuts of almost 5 percent and convinced the legislature to pass pension reforms. Jerry Brown hasn't won all his battles, but he has enjoyed support in public opinion polls at levels far greater than support for the legislature.

Ever-Changing Relationships

The powers of the governor's office remain basically the same year after year and administration after administration. But how those powers are managed depends on the issues, the times, the political environment, and the personality of the occupant. Yet one fact remains indisputable: the governor is clearly first among equals in the executive branch.

THE SUPPORTING CAST

Most states provide for the election of a lieutenant governor, a secretary of state, a treasurer, and an attorney general, but few elect an education officer, a controller, a Board of Equalization, and an insurance regulator. Moreover, most states require the governor and the lieutenant governor (and others, in some cases) to run on the same party ticket, thus providing some cohesion. Not so in California, where each elected member of the executive branch is elected independently of the others.

The consequences can be quite serious. For example, when Governor Schwarzenegger unilaterally withheld $3.1 billion from the public schools in 2005 in defiance of what many believed were state guarantees, Superintendent of Public Instruction Jack O'Connell sued. Ultimately, O'Connell dropped the suit after the governor and public school officials found agreement. On another occasion, then-state Republican Insurance Commissioner Steve Poizner sued to stop the sale of the state-run workers' compensation insurance fund, proposed by fellow Republican Governor Arnold Schwarzenegger. The issue was dropped after Schwarzenegger and Poizner left office. These examples show the extent to which very public fights can occur between two independently operating office-holders in the executive branch.

The Lieutenant Governor

The **lieutenant governor** is basically an executive-in-waiting with few formal responsibilities. If the governor becomes disabled or is out of the state, the lieutenant governor fills in as acting governor. If the governor leaves office, the lieutenant governor takes over. This has happened seven times in the state's history; most recently in 1953, when Goodwin Knight replaced Earl Warren, who became chief justice of the U.S. Supreme Court. The current lieutenant governor, Democrat and former San Francisco mayor Gavin Newsom, was elected in 2010, displacing Abel Maldonado, who had been appointed to the office earlier in the year.

The lieutenant governor heads some units, such as the State Lands Commission and the Commission on Economic Development, and is an ex officio member of the University of California Board of Regents and California State University Board of Trustees. He or she also serves as president of the state senate, but this job, too, is long on title and short on substance. As senate president, the lieutenant governor may vote to break 20-20 ties, an event that last occurred in 1976. So minimal are the responsibilities of the lieutenant governor; one occupant once quipped his biggest daily task was to wake up, check the morning newspaper to see whether the governor had died, and then return to bed![12] That description may stretch the point a bit, but not by much. As current Lieutenant Governor Newsom recently said about the office, "it's just so dull."[13]

The Attorney General

Despite the lieutenant governor's higher rank, the **attorney general** is usually considered the second-most powerful member of the executive branch. As head of the Department of Justice, the attorney general oversees law enforcement activities, acts as legal counsel to state agencies, represents the state in important cases, and renders opinions on (interprets) proposed and existing laws. In the 2010 contest for attorney general, former San Francisco district attorney Kamala Harris narrowly defeated Los Angeles County District Attorney Steve Cooley for the position. She succeeded Jerry Brown, who served between 2006 and 2010. Harris is also the first female and person of color to hold the post.

Substantial authority and independent election allow the attorney general to chart a course separate from the governor on important state questions. During his tenure as attorney general, for example, Jerry Brown sued insurance companies for misleading ads, prosecuted companies for not paying at least the minimum wage, and petitioned the federal government to regulate greenhouse gases.

Harris has made her own mark. In 2011, she resisted going along with a $20 billion settlement of a suit accepted by forty-eight other states against five major banks for abusive practices. But Harris held out, arguing that Californians would be short-changed. A few months later, the banks agreed to settle at $32 billion, enabling California to gain a much larger share of the disbursement.[14]

The Secretary of State

Unlike the U.S. cabinet official who bears the same title, the **secretary of state** of California is basically a records keeper and elections supervisor. The job entails certifying the number and validity of signatures obtained for initiatives, referenda, and recall petitions; producing sample ballots and ballot arguments for the voters; publishing official election results; and keeping candidate campaign finance records. The current secretary of state, Democrat Debra Bowen, was first elected in 2006. She has brought order to an office that was rocked by scandal in 2005, when then secretary of state Kevin Shelley resigned because of receiving illegal campaign contributions.

Recently, the secretary of state has had responsibility for converting California's election system from paper ballots to electronic voting machines. Bowen, a skeptic about electronic voting, has been in no great hurry. In 2007 she announced a ban on almost all electronic voting machines in thirty-nine counties until it could be demonstrated that the machines are not prone to any viruses or manipulation. This policy has required counties to either invest in new state-certified machines that include paper verification or resort to paper ballots.

The Superintendent of Public Instruction

The **superintendent of public instruction** heads the Department of Education. He or she is the only elected official in the executive branch chosen by nonpartisan ballot. Unless one candidate wins a majority in the June primary, the top two candidates face each other in the November general election. The superintendent's powers are severely limited. Funding is determined largely by the governor's budgetary decisions, and policies are closely watched by the governor-appointed state board of education and the education committees of the legislature.

In general, the electorate knows little about the office, but teachers' unions, education administrators, and other affected groups take great interest in the choice of superintendent because this official is the advocate for California's massive public education system. The current superintendent of public instruction, former state senator and assemblyman Tom Torlakson, was elected in 2010 with strong support from the California Teachers' Association, the most powerful education organization in the state.

The Money Officers

Perhaps the most fractured part of the executive branch of California government is the group of elected officials who manage the state's money. Courtesy of the Progressive reformers who feared a concentration of power, the controller, the treasurer, and the Board of Equalization have separate but overlapping responsibilities in this area. The **controller** supervises all state and local tax collection and writes checks for the state, including those to state employees. The controller is also an *ex officio* (automatic, by virtue of the office) member of several agencies, including the Board of Equalization, the Franchise Tax Board, and the State Lands Commission. Of all the "money officers," the controller is the most powerful, and thus the most prominent. The current controller, Democrat and former Board of Equalization member John Chiang, was elected in 2006 in his first run for statewide office and reelected in 2010. He has been an outspoken critic of California's ongoing budget crisis.

The **treasurer** invests state funds raised through taxes and other means until they are needed for expenditures. The treasurer also borrows money for the state by issuing bonds approved by the voters. Typically amounting to several billion dollars, the bonds are sold in financial markets to permit development of long-term projects such as highways, water projects, or other infrastructure needs. The state then "redeems" the bonds over time through interest payments. Democrat Bill Lockyer, former state attorney general, was elected to this office in 2006 and reelected in 2010. He has gained some notoriety by publishing periodic reports that reflect on the state's financial status with lending institutions that purchase California bonds.

The **Board of Equalization**, also part of California's fiscal system, oversees the collection of excise taxes on sales, gasoline, and liquor. The board also reviews county property assessment practices to ensure uniform calculation methods and practices. The board has five members—four of whom are elected in districts of equal population, plus the controller. Historically, the board has attracted little attention, but in 2007 the members voted to tax "alcopops"—sweet alcohol drinks often consumed by underage drinkers—at the same rate as hard liquor instead of beer. The change would have raised the tax from 20 cents per gallon to $3.30 per gallon, increasing the cost of alcopop drinks by about 25 percent. But manufacturers avoided the tax by lowering the alcohol content.

The Insurance Commissioner

The office of **insurance commissioner** exemplifies the persistent reform mentality of California voters. Until 1988, the office was part of the state's Business, Housing, and Transportation Agency. However, with soaring insurance rates, voters approved an initiative that called for 20 percent across-the-board reductions in automobile insurance premiums and created the elected position of insurance commissioner. Consumer Watchdog, the public interest group behind the proposition, claims that the law saved California drivers more than $60 billion during its first twenty years of existence.

Democrat Dave Jones, a termed-out member of the state assembly, was elected to the office in 2010, succeeding Steve Poizner, who unsuccessfully sought the Republican nomination for governor. Jones campaigned with the promise to hold health insurance companies accountable for any rate increases, an authority not held by the commissioner. However, with the passage of the Affordable Care Act by Congress, most observers expect the legislature to give this responsibility to Jones, as is the case in thirty other states.

The Supporting Cast—Snow White's Seven Dwarfs?

Combined, the seven other elected members of the executive branch (plus the Board of Equalization) present an appearance of tremendous political activity. Still, their efforts often center on narrow policy areas and frequently are in opposition to one another, as well as to the much more powerful governor.

THE BUREAUCRACY

Elected officials are just the most observable part of the state's administrative machinery. Backing them up, implementing their programs, and dealing with citizens on a daily basis are about 341,000 state workers—the **bureaucracy**. Only about 5,000 of these workers are appointed by the governor or by other executive officers. The remainder are hired and fired through the state's **civil service system** on the basis of their examination results, performance, and job qualifications. The Progressives designed this system to insulate government workers from political influences and to make them more professional than those who might be hired out of friendship.

The task of the bureaucracy is to carry out the programs established by the policymaking institutions: the executive branch, the legislature, and the judiciary, along with a handful of regulatory agencies. However, because bureaucrats are permanent, full-time professionals, they sometimes influence the content of programs and policies, chiefly by advising public officials or by exercising the discretion built into the laws that define bureaucratic tasks. The bureaucracy can also influence policy through the lobbying efforts of its employee organizations (see Chapter 4).

State bureaucrats work for various departments and agencies (see Figure 7.1), each run by an administrator who is appointed by the governor and confirmed by the senate. Sometimes, political appointees and civil servants clash over the best ways to carry out state policy. If the bureaucracy becomes too independent, the governor can always use his or her budgetary powers to bring it back into line or, in some cases, dismiss appointees.

In recent years, California's bureaucrats have been particularly ambitious on climate change. The California Energy Commission (CEC) has instituted energy efficiency standards for televisions and other electrical appliances. Also, the

California Air Resources Board (CARB) has led the way in regulating greenhouse gas levels. These efforts have kept California's energy consumption flat during the past three decades, compared with a 40 percent increase in energy consumption nationwide. They have also established California as a trendsetting state on the issues of global warming and energy use.

Some observers have criticized California's bureaucracy as unnecessarily inflated and unresponsive, even though the size of the state's system ranks forty-eighth of the fifty states on a per capita basis.[15] Still, there is no denying that slim or not, the state's bureaucracy grew under the Schwarzenegger administration to about 350,000, despite his promise to "blow up the boxes" of the bureaucracy shortly after taking office. Under Governor Jerry Brown, the size of the state bureaucracy has actually declined by nearly 10,000 employees, as he and the legislature have struggled to find ways to reduce the cost of state government. Brown has also successfully promoted pension reform, which reduces the state's obligations to state government retirees.

MAKING THE PIECES FIT

The executive branch is a hodgepodge of independently elected authorities who serve in overlapping and conflicting institutional positions. Nobody, not even the governor, is really in charge. Each official simply attempts to carry out his or her mission with the hope that passable policy will result. Occasionally, reformers have suggested streamlining the system by consolidating functions and reducing the number of elective offices, but the only relative recent change has been the addition of yet another office, that of insurance commissioner.

Despite these obstacles, the officeholders—most notably governors—have been active policymakers. Pete Wilson waged war against illegal immigrants, affirmative action, and welfare while trumpeting "law and order." Gray Davis responded to the state's power shortage crisis. Arnold Schwarzenegger was instrumental in environmental reform. And Jerry Brown has championed "efficiency," perhaps more out of necessity than desire.

Still, the governor does not operate in a vacuum. He or she must contend with other members of the executive branch, a fractured and suspicious legislature, independent courts, a professional bureaucracy, and most of all, an electorate with a highly erratic collective pulse. Whether these conditions are challenges or impediments, they make the executive branch a fascinating element of California government.

NOTES

1. "Special Sessions Define Schwarzenegger," *Sign on San Diego*, October 22, 2009, http://signonsandiego.printthis.clickability.com/pt/cpt?action=cpt&tit.

2. "Gov. Jerry Brown Orders California Workers to Turn in 48,000 Cellphones," *Los Angeles Times*, January 12, 2011, http://articles.latimes.com/print/2011/jan/12/local/la-me-cell-phones-20110112.

3. "Tensions Flare between Davis and His Democrats," *Los Angeles Times*, July 22, 1999, pp. A1, A28.

4. "Davis Comments Draw Fire," *San Jose Mercury News*, March 1, 2000, p. 14A.

5. *The Field Poll*, Release #2074, July 15, 2003.

6. For an account of how Davis fell from power, see Larry N. Gerston and Terry Christensen, *Recall! California's Political Earthquake* (Armonk, N.Y.: M. E. Sharpe, 2004).

7. "Gov. Criticizes Legislators as 'Girlie Men,'" *Los Angeles Times*, July 18, 2004, pp. B1, B18.

8. "Governor Slashes Workers' Pay," *San Francisco Chronicle*, July 2, 2010, pp. C1, C6.

9. "Schwarzenegger's Popularity Slide," *Los Angeles Times*, October 28, 2005, p. B2.

10. "Schwarzenegger Says the Fault Is His," *New York Times*, November 11, 2006, p. A14.

11. "Policymaking on Hold as Brown Nurses His Wounds," *Los Angeles Times*, August 17, 2011, pp. AA1, AA4.

12. "The Most Invisible Job in Sacramento," *Los Angeles Times*, May 10, 1998, pp. A1, A20.

13. "Uh, Gavin…," *San Francisco Chronicle*, May 31, 2012, p. A15.

14. "Rising Star Mixes Idealism, Political Savvy," *San Francisco Chronicle,* April 29, 2012, pp. A1, A12.

15. "Looking for Waste," *Economist*, May 1, 2010, p. 33.

LEARN MORE ON THE WEB

Office of the Attorney General:
www.caag.state.ca.us

Office of the Governor:
www.gov.ca.gov

Office of the Secretary of State:
www.ss.ca.gov

Office of the State Board of Equalization:
www.boe.ca.gov

Office of the State Controller:
www.sco.ca.gov

Office of the State Insurance Commissioner:
www.insurance.ca.gov

Office of the State Treasurer:
www.treasurer.ca.gov

Office of the State Superintendent of Public Instruction:
www.cde.ca.gov/eo

Salaries of state employees:
www.capitolweekly.net/salaries/index.php?_c=yzbexjathf9ge0

LEARN MORE AT THE LIBRARY

John C. Bollens and G. Robert Williams. *Jerry Brown in a Plain Brown Wrapper*. Pacific Palisades, Calif.: Palisades Publishers, 1978.

Larry N. Gerston and Terry Christensen. *Recall! California's Political Earthquake*. Armonk, N.Y.: M. E. Sharpe, 2004.

Gary G. Hamilton and Nicole Woolsey Biggert. *Governor Reagan, Governor Brown: A Sociology of Executive Power*. New York: Columbia University Press, 1984.

Joe Mathews. *The People's Machine*. New York: Public Affairs Press, 2006.

8

＊

Taxing and Spending: Budgetary Politics and Policies

CHAPTER CONTENTS

N o issue is more critical to Californians than taxation, and no resource is more important to state policymakers than the revenues generated from taxation. Those dollars become the foundation of the annual state budget, which determines where and how state funds will be spent.

The connection between taxing and spending can be difficult. Even though most people may agree on taxes in principle, they often disagree on how much should be collected and from whom, as well as the recipients of those funds. When policymakers seem to stray from general public values on budgetary issues, the voters are not shy about using direct democracy to reorder the state's fiscal priorities—and with so many more policy areas of need than dollars available, much is at stake.

CALIFORNIA'S BUDGET ENVIRONMENT

Unlike the national government, which usually operates with a deficit, state constitutions require balanced budgets. This has been difficult in California, where a steady flow of immigrants, a burgeoning school-aged population, massive attention to crime, and deteriorating infrastructure combine for a challenging budget environment. Since a recession in 2002, the state has struggled with one projected state revenue deficit after another regardless of who has been in power.

A deficit of more than $20 billion helped seal the fate of Governor Gray Davis in the unprecedented 2003 recall election. His replacement, Arnold Schwarzenegger promised fiscal soundness, and found himself victimized by California's unpredictable fiscal climate. In fact, his first budget was $8 billion out of balance immediately upon signature. A temporary economic upswing in 2006 facilitated a balanced, on-time budget for the first time in years. But the joy was short-lived.

By 2008, the state faced a revenue shortfall in excess of $15 billion, once again forcing drastic cuts. Twice in 2009, the governor and legislature grappled with the deficit. First, they sutured a massive $42 billion hole in March through a combination of new taxes, program cuts, and transfers. Three months later, state leaders had to overcome a new $24 billion gap, this time in program and services cuts only. The state's economic malaise persisted into the 2010–2011 fiscal year, when the weary governor and legislature faced a new $21 billion hole. Again they cut.

On his return to the state's office in 2011, Jerry Brown found himself haunted by the same environment that had plagued his predecessors. This time, the state faced a $26 billion deficit for the coming fiscal year, leading to more cuts in almost every program area except prisons. By 2012, an exasperated Governor Brown and the legislature plugged half of a $16 billion hole for the 2012–2013 fiscal year. But Brown warned there would be three fewer weeks in the school year if the voters did not pass a November initiative producing temporary tax increases of about $8 billion annually for seven years to generate the rest. They did. Even so, California's state budget has shrunk from about $105 billion in 2005–2006 to $91 billion in 2012–2013, as the state's population has grown from 36 million to 38.6 million.

The voters haven't helped with this ongoing dilemma. Repeatedly, the public has rejected new taxes while embracing new programs and services. When two Field polls in March 2010 asked the best way to balance the state budget, respondents who favored spending cuts outnumbered those who favored tax increases by a margin of nearly 4 to 1.[1] Yet when survey respondents were asked where the cuts should be made, majorities could be found in only two of fourteen major public policy areas—prisons and parks.[2] Moreover, over the past quarter century, voters have passed a series of ballot propositions directing the state to spend money on various programs ranging from longer prison sentences to more comprehensive public education without providing the funds. This is the political environment in which elected officials must make tough decisions.

THE BUDGETARY PROCESS

Budget making is a complicated and lengthy activity in California. Participants include the governor and various executive-branch departments, the legislature and its support agencies, the public (via initiative and referendum), and increasingly, the courts when judges uphold or overturn commitments made by the other policymakers.

The Governor and Other Executive Officers

Preparation of the annual budget is the governor's most important formal power. Other policymakers participate in the budgetary process, but no other individual has as much clout. The governor frames the document before it goes to the legislature and then has additional say afterward through use of the item veto. Given this unique power position, legislative leaders often negotiate with the chief executive over what he or she will accept long before the budget lands on the governor's desk.

During the summer and fall, the governor's director of finance works closely with the heads of state agencies. Supported by a staff of fiscal experts and researchers, the director of finance gathers and assesses information about the anticipated needs of each department and submits a "first draft" budget to the governor in late fall. The governor presents a refined version of this draft to the legislature the following January. The state constitution gives the legislature until June 15 to respond.

Legislative Participants

Upon receiving the budget in January, the legislature's leaders do little more than refer the document to the legislative analyst. Over the next two months, the legislative analyst and his or her staff scrutinize each part of the budget, considering needs, costs, and other factors. Often, the analyst's findings clash with those of the governor, providing the legislature with an independent source of data and evaluation.

Meanwhile, two key legislative units in each house—the appropriations committees and the budget committees—shepherd the budget proposal through the legislative process. After the staffs of these committees spend about two months scrutinizing the entire document, each house assigns portions to various other committees and their staffs. During this time, lobbyists, individual citizens, government officials, and other legislators testify on the proposed budget before committees and subcommittees. By mid-April, the committees conclude their hearings, combine their portions into a single document, and bring the budget bill to their respective full house for a vote.

As June nears and the two houses hone their versions, a select group of leaders enter into informal negotiations over the document. Known as the **Big Five**, the governor, the speaker of the assembly, the president pro tem of the senate, and the minority party leaders of each house become the nucleus of the final budgetary decisions. In recent years, the Big Five have cast long shadows over just about all of the other players. Should the two houses differ on specifics, the bill goes to a two-house conference committee for reconciliation, after which both houses vote again. With passage of **Proposition 25** in 2010, it now takes a simple majority to pass the budget, a change from the previous long-standing two-thirds requirement. However, inasmuch as a two-thirds vote is still required for revenue increases, the significance of this change is questionable.

The Courts

Sometimes, the courts weigh in on key budget issues to address some of the "quick fixes" to complex budget issues enacted by public policymakers or the voters. Governor Schwarzenegger was humbled in 2005 when a state superior court judge ruled that he was obligated to enforce a new law that reduced the ratio of patients to nurses from 6–1 to 5–1. In 2008, a decision by the U.S. District Court forced the state to spend billions of dollars on improved prison conditions, adding still more to a budget already billions in the red. In 2009 a federal court rejected $500 million in social service cuts as incompatible with federal law, a decision that added to the budget crisis of that year. And even as California attempted to comply with a federal court order to reduce the inmate population of its overcrowded state prisons, a court-appointed receiver rejected the state's effort to reduce costs as excessive. Clearly, the courts have found reason to shape state budgets.

Even the will of the voters has been subject to judicial review on matters relating to the state budget. Particularly significant have been the many cases arising from Proposition 13. Also, decisions on the death penalty and the famous "three strikes and you're out" initiative (see Chapter 6) have added greatly to state incarceration costs.

The Public

On occasion, the public shapes the budget through initiatives or referenda. The voters relied on ballot propositions to approve the sales tax (1933) and repeal the inheritance tax (1982).

In 1993 the voters passed a proposition that increased the state sales tax by 0.5 percent, with new revenues exclusively earmarked for public safety provided by local governments. In 2004 the voters enacted an initiative that created an additional 1 percent tax bracket for people with taxable incomes of $1 million or more, with the funds designated for mental health programs. And in 2012, the voters passed **Proposition 30**, which temporarily increased sales and income taxes for individuals with annual incomes over $250,000 to offset declining state revenues.

The public doesn't always agree to increases, however. The voters soundly rejected a 2006 initiative that would have added an additional tax bracket of 1.7 percent beyond the highest level for individuals with taxable incomes of $400,000 or more, with the revenues earmarked for a statewide preschool program.

In 2009, the governor and legislature strung together five ballot proposals that would simultaneously cap spending and temporarily increase sales taxes (0.25 percent), income taxes (1 percent), and motor vehicle fees (0.50 percent). The public said no to all five propositions.

Perhaps the most dramatic tax-altering event came in 1978 with the passage of **Proposition 13**, an initiative that reduced local property taxes by 57 percent. Since then, property owners have saved more than $528 billion in taxes,[3] while local governments have become increasingly dependent on the state for relief. As a result, the state has become the major funder for local services such as public education, although support has varied with the health of the economy. This uncertainty has brought endless criticism from local government officials.

The bottom line is that there are many more players in the budget process than meet the eye. This complexity both slows down the process and requires near unanimity among the various parties before any major decisions are made.

REVENUE SOURCES

Like most states, California relies on several forms of taxation for its general fund budget (that is, the budget exclusive of federal funds). The largest sources of revenue are personal income tax, sales tax, and bank and corporation taxes. Smaller revenue supplies come from motor vehicle, fuel, insurance, tobacco, and alcohol taxes. The state's major revenue sources and expenditures for fiscal year 2012–2013 are shown in Figure 8.1.

Other taxes are levied by local governments. Chief among these is the property tax, although its use was reduced considerably by Proposition 13. This tax is collected by counties rather than by the state, but the state allocates it among the different levels of local government, and it still is a part—directly or indirectly—of the tax burden of all Californians.

All too aware of the state's antitax mood, policymakers have refused to add taxes to cope with burgeoning needs. As a result, the state's commitments to most services have decreased considerably over the past three decades. Individual recipients, school districts, and local governments have been thrown into turmoil. Infrastructure projects, such as highway maintenance programs and Sacramento delta levee repairs, have been stretched out. Placement of a new earthquake-resistant Oakland–San Francisco Bay bridge will not be complete until 2013, twenty-four years after the earthquake that caused its damage. And

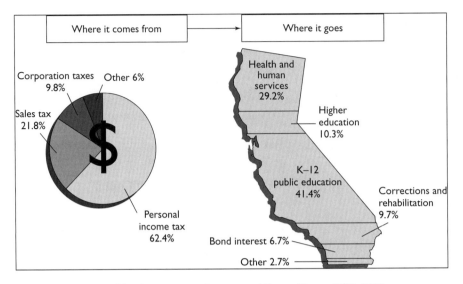

FIGURE 8.1   California's Revenue Sources and Expenditures, 2012–2013.
SOURCE: Legislative Analyst's Office

a recent study finds two-thirds of the state's roads in disrepair and 30 percent of the state's bridges "structurally deficient or fundamentally obsolete."[4]

The Sales Tax

Until the Great Depression of 1929, a relatively small state government garnered funds by relying on minor taxes on businesses and utilities. After the economic crash, however, the state was forced to develop new tax sources to cope with hard times. The first of these, a 2.5 percent **sales tax** on certain goods and products except food, was adopted to provide permanent funding for schools and local governments. Today, the statewide sales tax is 7.50 percent, courtesy of the one quarter addition that was part of Proposition 30. Of that amount, cities and counties get 2 percent to help meet health and public safety needs. The state keeps the rest. In addition, as much as 1.5 percent is tacked on by cities and counties engaged in state-approved projects, most of which are transportation related. Today, the sales tax accounts for about 21.8 percent of the state's tax revenues.

The Personal Income Tax

A second major revenue source, the personal income tax, was modeled after its federal counterpart to collect greater amounts of money from those residents with greater earnings. Today, the personal income tax varies between 1.0 and 12.3 percent, depending on one's income. The 11.3 percent and 12.3 percent brackets, however, have seven-year life spans for individuals earning between $350,000 and $500,000 and more than $500,000, as a result of Proposition 30.

The personal income tax is now the fastest-growing component of state revenue (see Figure 8.2)—a significant fact because Californians ranked eleventh

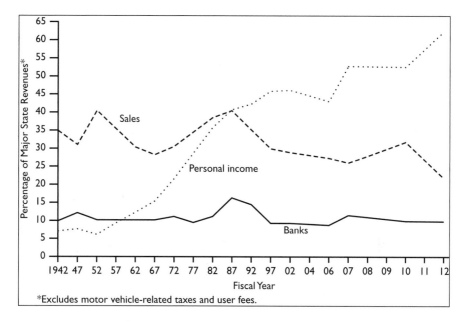

FIGURE 8.2 California's Tax Burden, 1942–2012.
SOURCE: Department of Finance

among the fifty states in per capita income in 2011. As of 2012, the personal income tax accounted for 62.4 percent of the state tax bite.

Corporation Taxes

Corporation income taxes contribute much less to California's budget than do sales and personal income taxes. Taxes on corporate incomes did not exceed 5.5 percent until 1959, when the legislature enacted the first of a series of rate hikes. Since 1996, the corporate tax rate has remained at 8.84 percent. Corporation taxes now account for about 9.8 percent of state revenues.

Aside from Proposition 13 and the reliance on **user taxes**, such as those levied on gasoline and cigarettes, California's revenue collection system has undergone gradual adjustments over the past sixty years. Figure 8.2 shows the changing weight of the sales, personal income, and corporation taxes from 1942 to the present. Along with a steady drift toward increased dependence on the personal income tax, the state has experienced decreased dependence on sales and corporation taxes.

Bonds

From time to time, state leaders have asked voters to approve bonds, thus obligating the electorate to long-term commitments. These projects, sometimes lasting as long as forty years, finance major infrastructure commitments such as school classroom, transportation, and water projects.

The state has turned to bonds with increasing frequency. In 1991, California ranked thirty-second among the fifty states in indebtedness on a per capita basis. By 2010, the state's bond debt increased to more than $140 billion, $70 billion of which had been enacted during the Schwarzenegger administration alone. That represents a per capita indebtedness of $2,362, second only to New York.

Taxes in Perspective

Viewed in a comparative context, the overall tax burden for California ranks ninth in the nation on a per capita basis, remarkably close to its per capita income ranking. Nevertheless, there have been changes in the state tax blend, with the state becoming increasingly dependent on the personal income tax as its primary source of income.

On a per capita basis, the state ranks third in personal income taxes, ninth in corporation taxes, twelfth in sales taxes, and twenty-ninth in property taxes.[5] In other areas, California taxes are near the bottom, due largely to the influence of powerful interest groups. For example, the state ranks forty-ninth in both fuel taxes and alcoholic beverage taxes. Reformers attempted to establish oil production taxes of $400 million over ten years via initiative in 2006, but the measure was soundly defeated at the polls. As a result, California is the only one of fourteen major oil-producing states that does not tax oil. With respect to tobacco taxes, California ranks thirty-third in the nation.[6] Had the voters approved a ballot proposition in 2012 increasing the tobacco tax by $1.00 per pack, the state would be collecting an additional $1 billion for children's health care, but that measure, too, was defeated. In these and other cases, interest groups have carried great sway with the legislature and public.

SPENDING

The annual state budget addresses thousands of financial commitments, both large and small. Major areas include public education (grades K through 12), health and welfare, higher education, and prisons. Outlays in these four areas account for nearly 90 percent of the general fund. The remainder of the budget (the difference between total expenditures and the general fund) goes to designated long-term projects such as transportation, parks, and veterans' programs, many of which have been authorized by public ballot or include federal funds.

Since 1979, several voter-passed ballot propositions have created a budget system that is largely formula-driven. K-12 public education, transportation programs, and mental health are among the many program areas where either percentages of the budget or specific revenues are directed for specific areas. Thus, public education receives at least 40 percent of the general fund unless two-thirds of the legislature grants a waiver because of a fiscal emergency. Likewise motor vehicle fees are directed exclusively for transportation-related services and projects. Some critics have characterized the formula approach as a political "straitjacket" that is unresponsive to changing times and needs. Defenders of "formula government" argue that it is the only way to keep state leaders from operating with a blank check.

Public Education: Grades K through 12

The state constitution gives public education a "superior right" to state funds; as such, public schools get the largest share of the state budget. Local school districts periodically add relatively small amounts to education through voter-approved bonds and parcel taxes, but the preponderance of support comes from the state legislature through its annual allocations.

Funding for public education in California has an uneven history. The state ranked among the top-funded states throughout the 1950s and 1960s. Then the pattern changed. During the 1970s and 1980s, the state consistently reduced its per capita support for K through 12 public education, shrinking it to 37 percent of the general fund in 1988. That same year, amid growing concerns about weak funding and poor classroom performance, education reformers secured voter approval of **Proposition 98**, a measure that established 40 percent as a minimum funding threshold except in times of fiscal emergency. With this mandate, the state poured money into reducing class sizes in grades K through 3 and lengthened the school year from 180 to 190 days. But the upward direction was short-lived.

State aid for public education has dropped precipitously with declining state revenues. Between 2008 and 2012 alone, support fell from $50.3 billion to $37.8 billion. At $9,908 per student (2011–2012 figures), California expenditures remain about $2,800 below the national average,[7] and thousands more below comparable industrialized states. According to former state superintendent of public instruction Jack O'Connell, California ranks forty-sixth of the fifty states in per capita expenditures, despite having one of the highest per capita incomes in the nation (see Figure 8.3).[8] Meanwhile, the school year minimum has fallen to 175 days, three full weeks less classroom instruction than fifteen years ago. Only four states require less attendance from their students.

California ranks fiftieth among the states in its student-teacher ratio, a commonly used criterion for assessing education effectiveness. The state also ranks forty-seventh in the number of computers per classroom. All this has produced a sorry, if not unexpected, outcome in terms of high school graduation, where the state ranks forty-eighth.[9] According to studies by the National Assessment of Educational Progress, a well-known nonprofit group, California hovers near the bottom of almost every assessment category. Table 8.1 shows the most recent data available.

With Latino and Asian American students accounting for 51 percent and 12 percent of the school population, respectively, language-related issues have emerged. In 1998 the passage of **Proposition 227**, a measure limiting bilingual education for non-English-speaking students to one year, added to the debate over how to "mainstream" the diverse California student community. All of this has occurred in a state where one-fourth of all public school students are "English learners" (English is not the first language), compared with 9 percent nationally.

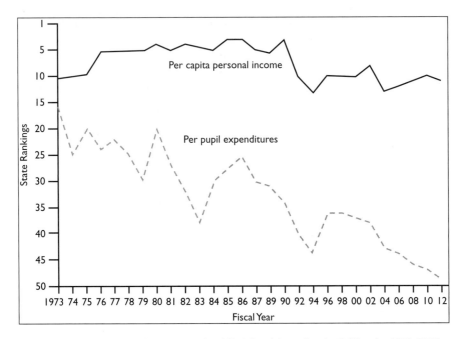

FIGURE 8.3 Personal Income and Public School Spending in California, 1973–2012.

TABLE 8.1 California Rankings in Key Education Categories

Category	Rank	Year
Reading, 4th grade	47th	2011
Reading, 8th grade	48th	2011
Math, 4th grade	44th	2011
Math, 8th grade	46th	2011
Science, 8th grade	48th	2011

SOURCE: National Assessment of Education Progress, 2012.

There are chilling consequences from these policies. For starters, California has a high school dropout rate of 24 percent, or about 125,000 students annually.[10] With few skills, their futures are very limited. At the other end of the spectrum, large numbers of those who do graduate high school are unprepared for college. A California State University study found that 55 percent of the incoming freshman class needed remedial instruction in either English or math.[11] Neither of these statistics points to educational excellence.

Nevertheless, the debate goes on. Some reformers have turned to "charter schools"—independent, community-controlled alternatives to what many describe as a broken system. As of 2012, there were about nine hundred charter schools in California, still a small number compared with the state's 9,700 traditional public schools, although up from six hundred in 2008. Other reformers have promoted vouchers—cash payments for parents to use in selecting an educational institution—but the voters have rejected such measures twice in recent years.

The process of fixing California's K-12 public education problems will be neither quick nor cheap. In 2007 a 1,700-page report commissioned by Governor Arnold Schwarzenegger declared that it would cost a staggering $1.5 trillion more each year to make all students academically proficient in traditional core knowledge areas such as reading, math, and science.[12] With current state, local, and federal expenditures for public education in the neighborhood of $75 billion, even the first step in such a leap would seem highly unlikely.

Higher Education: Colleges and Universities

California's budget woes have cut deeply into support for higher education. Once viewed as the role model for public universities,[13] the higher education system has suffered for a lack of funding and greatly reduced admission slots.

Three components share responsibility for higher education in the state. The state's 112 two-year community colleges enroll about 2.6 million students. Historically, community colleges have been viewed as the entry institutions for students who otherwise did not qualify for, or who could not afford to attend, California's four-year public universities. They also provide valuable training programs. Funding for community colleges is connected to the formula for primary and secondary public schools; to that extent, they have benefited from Proposition 98. Still, reduced budget allocations from the state have forced the community colleges to pare back instruction offerings. Between 2009 and 2012, state support dropped by 13 percent, while the number of course offerings fell by 10 percent. Meanwhile, student fees increased to $36 per unit from $26 per unit. As a result, community college enrollments have dropped by 300,000.[14]

With 222,000 students, the University of California (UC) educates both undergraduate and graduate students at ten campuses throughout the state. Designated as the state's primary research university, UC is the only public institution permitted to award professional degrees (such as medical and law degrees) and doctorates. The California State University (CSU) system, with 417,000 students at twenty-three campuses, concentrates on undergraduate instruction, awarding master's degrees most commonly in such fields as education, engineering, and business.

State support for public universities was fairly constant until the 1990s, holding at about 11 percent of the general fund budget, and it peaked at 12.7 percent during the 2002–2003 fiscal year. Support has eroded considerably since those heady days. For fiscal year 2012–2013, only 10.3 percent of the general fund was dedicated to the public universities. More significantly, the state's share of the cost of education has decreased dramatically. For example, whereas California provided 90 percent of UC's education costs in 1969–1970, support dropped less than half by 2010. And at CSU, the 90 percent paid by the state in 1969–1970 fell to 54 percent in 2011–2012. Students have been forced to make up the shortfall. At both UC and CSU, student fees have more than tripled between 2003–2004 and 2011–2012. Meanwhile, CSU has cut back new enrollments by 40,000; UC has reduced enrollments by 1,500. Between tuition increases and the lack of room, the college participation rate of nineteen-year-olds has fallen precipitously—from 22 percent to 18 percent between 2007 and 2012 alone, dropping California from seventeenth to forty-sixth place among the fifty states.[15]

Health and Human Services

Health and human services programs receive the second-largest share of the state budget. The programs accounting for the most significant state commitment include California Work Opportunity and Responsibility to Kids (CalWORKS), Medi-Cal, and the Supplemental Security Income (SSI) program. Medi-Cal provides health-care benefits for the poor, and SSI offers state assistance to the elderly and the disabled. But no program is as politically charged as CalWORKS, the primary welfare program.

California has sizable welfare costs. With about 12 percent of the nation's population, the state is home to 25 percent of all welfare recipients. In 1990, in contrast, California had 10.5 percent of the nation's population and 12 percent of all welfare recipients.

As welfare numbers have increased, per capita spending has gone down. Changes in state policy began in 1997 after Congress passed the Welfare Reform Act, limiting welfare payments to no more than five years. Shortly thereafter, the legislature passed its CalWORKS legislation, which provides cash grants and welfare-to-work services for needy families with children ten years of age or younger and requires all adults to work at least thirty-two hours per week. The eligibility period was reduced to four years under the Schwarzenegger administration. As of 2011, about 1.1 million Californians were CalWORKS recipients, two-thirds of whom were children.

In 2012, health and human services programs accounted for about 29.2 percent of the general fund. Average monthly welfare payments were $460 for the typical family of three, down by one-fourth from a decade earlier. Still, with the state scrambling to close a $16 billion budget hole for the coming fiscal year, Governor Brown and the legislature cut the eligibility period for CalWORKS recipients to two years, saving $880 million.

Prisons

Of the major state allocation categories, the budgets for prisons and corrections have grown the most in recent years. As with education, the public has played a role in this policy area. Several initiatives have established mandatory prison terms for various crimes and extended the terms for many other crimes. The most sweeping changes occurred in 1994, when the legislature (and later the voters, through an initiative) enacted a new **"three strikes"** law for repeat felons. As of 2012, about 9,000 of the state's 130,000 prisoners were incarcerated under the three-strikes classification.

As a result of the three-strikes law and other policy changes, California's prison population swelled beyond belief. In 1994 the total prison population was 125,000. It had jumped to 168,000 by 2009, with the cost for incarceration averaging $49,000 per convict per year. The demographics are equally interesting: 37 percent Latino, 27 percent African American, and 27 percent white. Phenomenal incarceration growth has forced the construction of new prisons. Still, with a soaring inmate population, in 2006 Governor Schwarzenegger asked the legislature to build at least two more state prisons at a cost of $500 million each.

Between 1994 and 2012, corrections and rehabilitation was the fast growing area of state spending, ultimately reaching 10 percent of the annual budget. But prisoner lawsuits on overcrowding and medical conditions resulted in the federal courts ordering the state to reduce the number of inmates by at least 40,000 inmates to better match the prison population with prison capacity. Governor Jerry Brown responded to the order by creating a program to move 30,000 of the state's least violent offenders to county jails with the promise of state funds to accompany the shift. Under his plan known as **realignment**, sentencing and parole protocols were altered to permit more inmates either in county jails or out under local supervision. Also in 2012, the voters passed **Proposition 36**, which made it easier for about 3,000 nonviolent offenders to request reduced sentences. The new policy reduced state spending on incarceration to 9.7 percent of the state budget by 2012–2013, with an anticipated reduction to 7.5 percent by 2015–2016. Still, local officials remained skeptical of its success, given their new responsibilities.[16]

Other Budget Obligations

California's budget crisis has many sources, some obvious and others not. Clearly, a prolonged recession has contributed mightily to the state's revenue grief. On the expenditure side of the budget ledger, out-of-control prison spending and welfare costs have been of great concern. Two other less known, yet fast-growing state expenditure categories are payment of bond debt and pension payouts. Together, they now consume close to 10 percent of the state general fund and show little sign of slowing down.

Bonds.   While voter-approved borrowing through bonds represents an "easy" way to fund major projects over time, cumulatively these bonds are taking a toll on the state. California now ranks tenth among the states in per capita bond debt, up from thirty-second in 1991. Our propensity to rely upon bonds has generated the lowest credit rating of any state, which adds to the interest costs to retire the bonds. About 6.7 percent of the state budget now goes to paying interest on the debt. Moreover, State Treasurer Bill Lockyer estimated in 2009 that at present rates, 10 percent or more of the state budget will be dedicated to debt payment by the middle of this decade.[17] The state's propensity for financing through bonds has left it with the lowest bond rating of any state, which means the highest interest payments.

Retirement Pensions.   California's massive public employee pension program, the California Public Employees' Retirement System (CalPERS), covers more than 1.6 million employees, retirees, and their families, or about 4 percent of the state's population. Just over 500,000 are retirees who have worked for various state government agencies. Employees contribute a small portion of their salary to the program, with the state providing the rest as part of the salary compensation package. For years CalPERS gushed with surpluses, thanks to a robust financial market that contained most of the fund's investments. Since the onslaught of the recession in 2008, CalPERS payments have exceeded revenues. By law, the state must make up for any shortfall, and that money comes out of the state budget. In fiscal year 2011–2012, the state was required pay out $2 billion of the general fund into CalPERS—double the amount paid in 2006. Because of spiraling costs, Governor Jerry Brown and the legislature enacted new cost control legislation in 2012, requiring higher employee contributions and extending retirement ages.

CALIFORNIA'S BUDGET: TOO LITTLE, TOO MUCH, OR JUST RIGHT?

Have you ever met anyone who claims that he or she should pay more taxes? Neither have we. Almost everybody dislikes paying taxes, and almost everybody thinks that the money collected is spent incorrectly or unwisely. That seems to be a perennial dilemma in California. However, although most people oppose increased taxes, they also oppose program cuts. It's a modern-day dilemma for state policymakers and the public alike.

Like their counterparts elsewhere, California policymakers have struggled to find a fair system of taxation to pay for needed programs. Given the involvement of so many public and private interests, however, it's difficult to determine what is fair. Moreover, during the last few decades, taxation and budget decisions have been subject to radical change. Somehow, the state's infrastructure has survived, although critics have been less than thrilled with the fiscal uncertainty that has become commonplace in California government.

NOTES

1. Field Poll, Release No. 2329, March 2, 2010.

2. Field Poll, Release No. 2335, March 24, 2010.

3. Howard Jarvis Taxpayers Association, 2009, www.hjta.org/index.php.

4. Tax Foundation, "Tax Data: California, March 3, 2011, http://www.taxfoundation .org/taxdata/show/228.html; "National and State Corporate Income Tax Rates, U.S. States and OECD Countries 2011," http://taxfoundation.org/article /national-and-state-corporate-income-tax-rates-us-states-and-oecd-countries-2011;

"Ranking State and Local Taxes," September 22, 2011, http://taxfoundation.org/article/ranking-state-and-local-sales-taxes-1, "Finance," in *Governing: State and Local Government Sourcebook* (Washington, D.C.: Congressional Quarterly, 2006), pp. 32–36.

5. "A Decade of Disinvestment: California Education Spending Nears the Bottom," California Budget Project, Sacramento, Calif., October 2011, p. 1.

6. "State Cigarette Excise Tax Rates and Rankings, 2012," www.tobaccofreekids.org.

7. Testimony before Assembly Budget Subcommittee No. 2, March 11, 2008.

8. *See Just the Facts* (Albany: Public Policy Institute of New York State, 2007).

9. "More Kids Staying in School," *San Francisco Chronicle*, June 28, 2012, pp. C1, C5.

10. "CSU Freshmen Face Challenges," *Los Angeles Times*, March 15, 2006, p. B9.

11. "No Quick, Cheap Fix for State's Schools," *Los Angeles Times*, March 15, 2007, pp. B1, B10.

12. See James Richardson, "What Price Glory?" *UCLA Magazine*, February 1997, p. 30; also see "A Crown Jewel of Education Struggles with Cuts in California," *New York Times*, November 20, 2009, pp. A1, A25.

13. "Colleges' Chancellor to Step Down," *Los Angeles Times*, March 7, 2012, p. AA3.

14. See Hans Johnson, "Defending Higher Education," Public Policy Institute of California, San Francisco, Calif., May 2012, pp. 7–8, and Christopher Neufeld and Stanton Glantz, "Ending the California Dream," op-ed in *San Francisco Chronicle*, July 14, 2009, p. A11.

15. "Counties Brace for Stream of State Prisoners," *San Francisco Chronicle*, October 2, 2011, pp. A1, A14.

16. "Rising Debt a Threat to State General Fund," *San Francisco Chronicle*, November 24, 2009, p. C3.

17. "California Bond Rating Now Lowest of Any State," *Los Angeles Times*, February 4, 2009, pp. A1, A11.

LEARN MORE ON THE WEB

California Budget Project:
www.cbp.org

California state budget—Department of Finance:
www.dof.ca.gov

California state budget—Legislature:
www.lao.ca.gov

California Tax Reform Association:
www.caltaxreform.org

California Taxpayers' Association:
www.caltax.org

National Center for Education Statistics:
www.nces.ed.gov

National Governors Association:
www.nga.org

LEARN MORE AT THE LIBRARY

Jack Citrin and Isaac William Martin, eds. *After the Revolt: California's Proposition 13*. Berkeley, Calif.: Berkeley Public Policy Press, 2009.

John Decker. *California in the Balance: Why Budgets Matter*. Berkeley, Calif.: Berkeley Public Policy Press, 2009.

Larry N. Gerston, *Not So Golden After All: The Rise and Fall of California*. New York, Taylor & Francis, 2012.

Alvin Rabushka and Pauline Ryan. *The Tax Revolt*. Stanford, Calif.: Hoover Institution Press, 1982.

Peter Schrag. *California: America's High-Stakes Experiment*. Berkeley: University of California Press, 2006.

9

California's Local Governments: Politics at the Grassroots

CHAPTER CONTENTS

News media tend to focus on state and national politics, but the activities of local governments often have a greater impact on our daily lives. Our city governments make decisions about traffic on our streets; safety in our neighborhoods; and access to parks, libraries, and affordable housing. Our county governments manage transit systems and provide important social services to those most in need, including people who are homeless, mentally ill, and impoverished. Our school districts decide what sorts of teachers are in our classrooms and what our children are taught.

Yet local governments are created by the state, which assigns them their rights and duties, mandating some responsibilities and prohibiting others. The state also allocates taxing powers and shares revenues with local governments. But the state can change the rights and powers granted to local governments, expanding or reducing their tasks, funding, and independence. Cities and counties are infuriated when the state tells them to do things they don't think they can afford or takes away previously committed funds to balance the state budget. School districts depend on the state for funding but are exasperated by burdensome state rules, regulations, and testing requirements.

Yet local government is also where we have the greatest influence over our lives, simply because we are closer to it than to Sacramento or Washington, D.C. We can participate directly in local politics precisely because it's local. We can volunteer for candidates, whom we can actually meet and get to know or even run for office ourselves. We can lobby elected officials without relying on paid professionals. We can attend city council meetings and testify in person. We can find allies and form interest groups like those described in Chapter 4 (and all those types exist in communities). Local government is the most democratic of all levels of government, and thousands of people participate constantly—go to your own city hall and see for yourself.

COUNTIES AND CITIES

California's 58 counties and 482 cities were created in slightly different ways and perform distinctly different tasks.

Counties

California is divided into counties (see the map inside the front cover) ranging in size from San Francisco's 47 square miles to San Bernardino County's 20,164, and ranging in population from Alpine County's 1,102 residents to Los Angeles County's 9,889,056. **Counties** function both as local governments and as administrative units of the state. As local governments, counties provide police and fire protection, maintain roads, and perform other services for rural and unincorporated areas (those that are not part of any city). They also run jails; operate transit systems; protect health and sanitation; and keep records on property, marriages, and deaths. As agencies of the state, counties oversee elections, operate the courts, administer the state's welfare system, and collect some taxes. The responsibilities of counties were expanded in 2012, when Governor Jerry Brown's **realignment** program assigned incarceration of nonviolent felons from prisons to county jails, a cost saving for the state even with reimbursement of the cost to counties. Some counties complained, however, that their reimbursements don't cover the costs of realignment and others fear they'll be in the same situation in the future.

State law prescribes the organization of county government. A county's central governing body is a five-member **board of supervisors**, whom voters elect by districts to staggered four-year terms. The board sets county policies and oversees the budget and usually hires a chief administrator, or **county executive**, to carry out its programs. Besides the members of the board of supervisors, voters

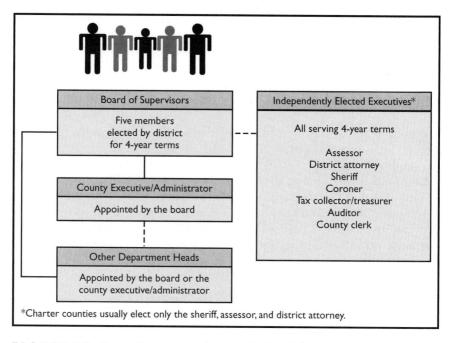

FIGURE 9.1 County Government: An Organizational Chart for California's Forty-four General Law Counties

elect the sheriff, district attorney, tax assessor, and sometimes other department heads (see Figure 9.1). Conflicts often occur as the elected board tries to manage the budget and the elected executives attempt to deliver services. Unlike most of their state counterparts, these local officials are chosen in nonpartisan elections, a Progressive legacy that keeps party labels off the ballot; all serve four-year terms. As of 2010, California's 296 elected county supervisors were overwhelmingly white and male; only 23.5 percent were female, 9.5 percent were Latino, 3.4 percent were Asian, and 1.7 percent were African American.

Although most counties operate under this general-law system, fourteen have used a state-provided option to organize their own governmental structures through documents called **charters**. Most of these charter counties, including Los Angeles, Sacramento, San Diego, and Santa Clara, are highly urbanized. County voters must approve the charter and any proposed amendments. Generally, a "home rule" or **charter county** uses its local option to replace elected executives with appointees of the board of supervisors or to strengthen the powers of the appointed county executive.

San Francisco is unique among California's local governments because it operates as both a city and a county. Most counties have several cities within their boundaries, but the separate city and county governments of San Francisco were consolidated in 1911. San Francisco thus has a board of supervisors with eleven members rather than a city council, but unlike any other county, it has a mayor.

No new county has been formed in California since 1907, although in some large counties such as Los Angeles, San Bernardino, and Santa Barbara, rural areas frustrated by urban domination have tried unsuccessfully to break away and form their own jurisdictions.

Cities

Whereas counties are created by the state, **cities** are established at the request of their citizens through the process of **incorporation**. Starting with just 8 cities in 1850, California has 482 today. As unincorporated areas urbanize, residents begin to demand more services than their county government can provide. These may include police and fire protection, street maintenance, water, or other services. Residents may also wish to form a city to preserve the identity of their community or to avoid being annexed by some other city. Wealthy areas sometimes incorporate to protect their tax resources or their ethnic homogeneity from the impact of an adjacent big city and its economic and racial problems. Jurupa Valley in Riverside County, incorporated in 2011 with a population of 95,004, is California's newest city.

The process of incorporation starts with a petition from citizens who live in the area. Then the county's **local agency formation commission (LAFCO)** determines whether the area has a sufficient tax base to support city services and makes sense as an independent entity. If LAFCO approves, the county's board of supervisors holds a hearing, and then the voters of the proposed city approve or reject the incorporation.

Once formed, cities can grow by annexing unincorporated (county) territory. Sometimes, small cities that can't provide adequate services disband themselves by consolidating with an adjacent city. More rarely, residents of an existing city seek to de-annex, or secede. The San Fernando Valley and other parts of the city of Los Angeles have felt ignored by their city government and attempted to secede in 2002, but voters in the city as a whole, who must agree to any secession, rejected the plan.

Like California counties, most California cities operate under the state's general law, which prescribes their governmental structure. **General law cities** typically have a five-member **city council**, with members elected in nonpartisan elections for four-year terms. The council appoints a **city manager** to supervise daily operations; the manager, in turn, appoints department heads such as the police and fire chiefs (see Figure 9.2).

Cities with populations exceeding 3,500 may choose to write their own charters. A hundred and twenty-one California cities have done so. A **charter city** has more discretion in choosing the structure of its government than a general law city does, as well as somewhat greater fiscal flexibility and the freedom to set policies, provided that no state law supersedes them. All of California's largest cities have their own charters.

Even after incorporation, the county provides for courts, jails, social services, elections, tax collection, public health, and public transit, but once incorporated, a city takes on extensive responsibilities, including police and fire protection,

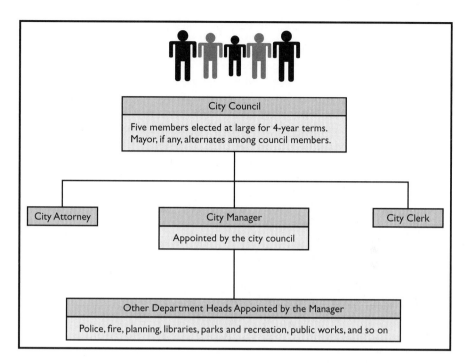

FIGURE 9.2 City Government: An Organizational Chart for California's 361 General Law Cities

sewage treatment, garbage disposal, parks and recreational services, streets and traffic management, library operation, and land use planning. The latter is arguably the greatest power given to cities. By zoning land for particular uses—housing, offices, shopping centers, or industry—city governments determine the nature of their communities as well as their financial resources, since some land uses generate more income than others.

POWER IN THE CITY: COUNCIL MEMBERS, MANAGERS, AND MAYORS

Most of California's cities have five-member city councils with appointed city managers as executives, as set forth by state law. Some cities, particularly older and larger communities, have developed municipal government structures uniquely suited to their own needs and preferences. City councils, for example, may be chosen in different ways or expanded in size to allow for more representation, particularly in larger cities. Los Angeles has fifteen council members, San Jose ten, and San Diego eight. San Francisco's board of supervisors has eleven members. The executive office also varies among these cities; some opt for a stronger mayor rather than the manager prescribed by the state for general law cities.

Elections

In most California cities, each council member is chosen by the whole city in **at-large elections**. This system was created by the Progressives to replace **district elections**, in which each council member represents only part of the city. At-large elections were intended to reduce the parochial influence of machine-organized ethnic neighborhoods on the city as a whole. The strategy worked, but as a result, ethnic minority candidates, unable to secure enough votes from the city as a whole to win at large, were rarely elected.

As cities grew, citywide campaigns also became extremely costly. The Progressives added to the difficulties of minority candidates and further raised the costs of campaigns by making local elections nonpartisan. This weakened the old party machines, but voters lost the modest cue provided by the listing of parties on the ballot.

To increase minority representation and cut campaign costs, some cities have returned to district elections. Los Angeles has used district elections since 1924; Sacramento converted in 1971, followed by San Jose, Oakland, Fresno, San Diego, and San Francisco. Thirty-eight California cities use some form of district elections. Most are large cities, and most have reverted to district elections through voter-approved charter amendments.

District elections increased opportunities for minority candidates in some cities, but minorities remain substantially underrepresented among California's local elected officials. Women and minority candidates, as well as gay and lesbian candidates, have been more successful in local elections than in state elections; they are still held back, however, by discrimination, low participation, at-large elections, and the cost of campaigns.

In most California cities, especially smaller cities that elect their councils at large, candidates who get the most votes win election even if they don't get a majority. In larger cities and cities that elect their council members by district, if no candidate wins a majority in the primary election, the top two compete in a **runoff election**, ensuring that the winner is elected with a majority. Critics object to the high cost of such elections—both to taxpayers and in campaign spending. In 2004 San Francisco responded to such criticism with **instant runoff voting**, in which voters rank their top three choices of candidates in order of preference. Oakland followed with the same system in 2010. If no candidate wins a majority, the candidate with the fewest votes is eliminated and those votes are assigned to the voters' second choice—and so on until one candidate attains a majority. In the 2010 mayoral election in Oakland, Don Perata, the candidate who won the most votes fell short of a majority and when the second and third choices votes were recorded Jean Quan was elected mayor—much to the chagrin of some voters. Supporters of this system hope that it saves time and money, but voters and candidates have experienced considerable confusion in its implementation.

Whatever the system, voter participation varies considerably from city to city. Turnout is generally higher in cities with elected mayors and district elections, but the key factor related to turnout is when the elections are held. About one-third of California's cities hold their elections separate from state and national elections.

Median turnout in these elections is less than 30 percent.[1] Los Angeles, for example, holds its elections separately, and turnout in that city's 2009 city council and mayoral contests was 18 percent, while turnout in San Francisco's 2011 mayoral election was only 39 percent. Lower turnout significantly affects outcomes because the composition of the electorate changes along with the number of voters; older, more affluent voters predominate, giving an advantage to more conservative candidates. Researchers report that in cities with low voter turnout, less money is spent on programs that might help the poor and more goes to downtown development and other projects that aid business. In short, local governments spend their revenues on those who vote.[2] Turnout in cities that hold their elections concurrently with state and national elections is nearly twice as high.[3] The Silicon Valley city of Santa Clara started holding local elections at the same time as state and national elections in 1988, and voter turnout went from 23–24 percent to 74 percent. Unlike cities, California counties hold their elections at the same time as the state and national elections. Voting for local officials may still be lower, however, due to "drop-off," with some voters declining to cast ballots because of lack of interest or information.

As with state-level campaigns, local reformers have been concerned about the costs of city and county races and the influence of money on politics. Spending on local campaigns has risen steadily since the 1980s, when professional campaign consultants and their techniques (see Chapter 3) became common in local races. One hundred and fifty-one California cities and counties have enacted local campaign-finance laws requiring disclosure of contributors and expenditures and sometimes limit contributions. In most cases, the data are available to the public online. Los Angeles and a few other cities restrict spending and provide limited public financing for campaigns. Even in these communities, however, candidates and interest groups raise and spend substantial sums on campaigns, often through independent expenditures.

Executive Power

Most people assume that mayors lead cities and have substantial power, but that's not usually the case in California communities. Because mayors were once connected with political machines, the Progressive reformers shifted executive authority to council-appointed city managers who were intended to be neutral, professional administrators. Most California cities use this **council-manager system**. While the manager administers the city's programs, appoints department heads, and proposes the budget, the council members alternate as mayor—a ceremonial post that involves chairing meetings and cutting ribbons.

San Francisco, however, uses a strong-mayor form of government, in which the mayor is elected directly by the people to a four-year term and holds powers similar to those of the president in the national system, including the veto, budget control, and appointment of department heads. High-profile mayors with these powers include Ediwn Lee of San Francisco and Jean Quan of Oakland, both of whom are of Chinese ancestry. Voters in Los Angeles gave their mayor enhanced authority, including the power to appoint forty-four department heads, when they approved a new charter in 1999. Mayor Antonio Villaraigosa thus exercises more authority than any of his predecessors. Fresno (in 1997), Oakland (in 1998), and San Diego (in 2005) have also switched to a strong-mayor form of government. Sacramento mayor Kevin Johnson has pushed for such a change in his city, but the city council has declined putting a charter amendment to the voters.

Many California cities have moved away from the pure council–manager system of government, however. While retaining their city managers, 149 California cities have revised the system so that the mayor is directly elected and serves a four-year term. Some have also increased the powers of their mayors, although they continue to sit as council members. Even without much authority, being a directly elected mayor brings visibility and influence. Mayors of San Jose, for example, exercise substantial clout despite their limited official power.

California mayors will probably continue to grow stronger, partly because of media attention but also due to the need for leadership in the tempest of city politics. Elected officials and community groups often complain about the inherent lack of direct accountability in the city manager form where the executive is somewhat insulated from the voters. Giving more authority to mayors and council members makes accountability more direct, but it may also decrease the professionalism of local government.

MORE GOVERNMENTS

In addition to cities and counties, California has thousands of other, less visible local governments (see Table 9.1). Created by the state or by citizens, they provide designated services and have taxing powers, mostly collecting their revenues as small portions of the property taxes paid by homeowners and businesses or by charging for their services. Yet except for school districts, most of us are unaware of their existence.

School Districts and Special Districts

In California, 1,050 local governments called school districts provide education. They are created and overseen by the state and governed by elected boards,

T A B L E 9.1 California's Local Governments, 2012

Type	Number
Counties	58
Cities	482
School districts	1,050
Special districts	4,792
TOTAL	6,382

SOURCE: California State Controller, www.sco.ca.gov, and Ed-Data, www.ed-data.ca.us.

which appoint professional educators as superintendents to oversee day-to-day operations. Except for parents and teachers, whose involvement is intense, voter participation in school elections and politics is low. One challenge for the schools is that while the majority of students are Latino, Asian, or African American, a majority of those who vote in school elections and most school board members are non-Hispanic whites.

Funding is another problem with revenues for schools down nearly 10 percent since the 2007–2008 budget year. Of the $56.7 billion in school spending in 2010–2011, the state supplied 58 percent, the federal government provided 14 percent, and 28 percent came from local property taxes and other local sources.[4] The decline in funding has not been without costs; California has ranked low among the states in per-pupil spending for years.[5] While the $56.7 billion goes to salaries and operating expenses, money for building repairs and construction of new schools comes mostly from **bonds** (borrowed money paid by local taxes), which require a supermajority of voters (55 percent) to approve—and usually get it.

Special districts are an even more common form of local government, with no fewer than 4,792 in California. Unlike cities and counties, which are "general-purpose" governments, special districts provide a single service. California law provides for fifty-three different types of special districts, ranging from water and waste disposal districts to hospital and cemetery districts. They are created when citizens or governments want a particular function performed but have no appropriate agency to provide the service or prefer not to delegate it to a city or county. Sometimes special districts are formed when small communities share responsibilities for fire protection, sewage treatment, or other services that can be more efficiently provided on a larger scale. When Proposition 13 passed in 1978, the number of special districts increased because that initiative imposed tax constraints on general-purpose local governments (cities and counties) and local leaders discovered that it was easier to fund some services through special districts. Depending on the nature of the special district, funding usually comes from property taxes or charges for the service it provides. Altogether, California's special districts spend over $40 billion a year, while California's cities spend $53 billion and its counties spend $57 billion.

A city council or a county board of supervisors governs some special districts, but most are overseen by a commission or board of directors that may be elected or appointed by other officials. Like a school board, this body usually appoints a professional administrator to manage its business. Accountability to the voters and taxpayers is a problem, however, because most of us aren't even aware of these officials.

Coping with So Many Governments

The existence of so many sorts of local governments means that many operate in every urban region of California. The vast urban areas between Los Angeles and San Diego or between San Francisco and San Jose, for example, consist of many cities, counties, and special districts, with no single authority in charge of the whole area. Los Angeles County alone hosts eighty-eight cities and two hundred special districts. This fragmentation creates small-scale governments that are accessible to citizens, but that are sometimes too small to provide services efficiently. In addition, problems such as transportation and air pollution go far beyond the boundaries of any one entity.

Many California cities deal with this situation by **contracting for services** from counties, larger cities, or private businesses. Cities in Los Angeles County, for example, may pay the county to provide any of fifty-eight services, from dog catching to tree planting. Small cities commonly contract with the county sheriff for police protection rather than fund their own forces. Contracting allows such communities to provide needed services while retaining local control, although some see the system as unfair because wealthy communities can afford more than poor ones.

Another solution to urban fragmentation is **consolidation**, or the merger of existing governmental entities. With voter approval, small school districts, special districts, or even cities can unite to provide services more efficiently. In the past, consolidation has occurred mostly with school districts, but proposals for consolidations have become more common lately due to California's prolonged budget crisis.[6]

Special districts are yet another way to address fragmentation and regional problems—particularly problems, such as air pollution and transportation, that extend beyond the boundaries of existing cities or counties. For example, California has forty-seven transit districts that run bus and rail systems. Most are countywide, but some, including the Bay Area Rapid Transit (BART) system, cover several counties.

As regional problems have grown and competition among cities has increased, the need for regional planning has also grown. The state has asserted its authority over local governments to require the implementation of regional plans through **councils of government (COGs)**, such as the Southern California Association of Governments (SCAG) and the nine-county Association of Bay Area Governments (ABAG) in Northern California, in which all of the cities and counties in the region are represented. Other state-created agencies, such as the Metropolitan Water District and the South Coast Air Quality Management Board in Southern California, also exercise great power.

DIRECT DEMOCRACY IN LOCAL POLITICS

Direct democracy is used even more locally than statewide. Between 1995 and 2011 an average of 402 local ballot measures were voted on by Californians each year.[7] Voters must approve all charter amendments—such as increasing the powers of the mayor or introducing district council elections. Proposals for local governments to introduce or raise taxes or to borrow money by issuing bonds must also win voter approval. Charter changes require a simple majority, but most tax increases require a two-thirds super majority. These requirements have severely restricted the ability of local governments to raise money, because voters are usually reluctant to increase taxes.

Most local measures are placed on the ballot by a city council, county board of supervisors, or school board. Besides tax measures and charter amendments, the most common measures have to do with schools (usually seeking additional funding). Citizens also put proposals to the voters through the initiative process, although initiatives constitute only a tiny percentage of local measures. Most often, the initiatives are attempts to control growth or amend charters. Some are frivolous, like the 2008 San Francisco initiative that proposed renaming the city sanitation facility the "George W. Bush Sewage Plant," but most are more serious. District elections, for example, were introduced in some cities by initiative, as were **term limits** (usually restricting elected officials to two 4-year terms). Several California counties and over forty cities now limit the terms of elected officials. As a last resort, voters may express their dissatisfaction with elected officials through recall elections. Recalls of local officials are rare, however, averaging fewer than a dozen a year.

A more frequent use of direct democracy in California communities has been by citizens seeking to control growth. Local government decisions about land use affect us all. If a local government encourages growth in the form of housing, industry, or shopping centers, for example, the economy may boom, but streets may become clogged, schools overcrowded, sewage treatment plants strained, and police and fire protection stretched too thin. Frustrated residents may demand controls on growth. If the city or county leaders are unresponsive, discontented groups may take their case to the voters through an initiative. Most California communities have enacted some form of growth control, with grassroots groups with little money battling big-spending developers and builders. This issue lost salience in recent years, however, when the recession halted growth in most places.

LOCAL BUDGETS

The way local governments raise and spend money reveals a great deal, not only about what they do but also about the limits they face in doing it.

The biggest single source of money for California's local governments was once the **property tax**, an annual assessment based on the value of land and buildings. Then, in 1978, taxpayers revolted with **Proposition 13**, a statewide initiative that cut property tax revenues by 57 percent. Cities adjusted by cutting jobs and services to save money. Many introduced or increased **charges for services** such as sewage treatment, trash collection, building permits, and the use of recreational facilities. Such charges are now the largest source of income for most cities (see Figure 9.3). Local governments also came to rely more on the state's 7.5 percent sales tax, 2 percent of which goes to the city or county where the sale occurs. Some cities and counties add to the base sales tax to fund transportation or other services. Some have also added taxes on hotel rooms, utilities, or other things such as Oakland's tax on the sale of medical marijuana.

The shift from property taxes to other sources of revenue also affects local land use decisions. When a new development is proposed, most cities now prefer retail businesses to housing or industry because of the sales taxes that such businesses generate. This trend has been labeled the **fiscalization of land use** because instead of choosing the best use for the land, cities opt for the one that produces the most revenue. Housing, especially affordable housing, never falls into this category.

With more legal constraints on their taxing powers, counties had an even rougher time after Proposition 13. State aid to counties increased slightly, but with no alternative local taxes readily available after the passage of Proposition 13, most counties cut spending deeply. Years later, they are still struggling to provide essential services. Like cities, most counties increased charges and fees for services.

Over half of county revenues come from the state and federal governments (33.3 percent and 22 percent, respectively), but this money must be spent on required programs such as social services, health care, and the courts. Even so, state and federal aid does not cover the cost of these mandatory services, leaving counties with little money to spend as they choose.

Just as the revenue sources of cities and counties differ, so do their spending patterns, largely because the state assigns them different responsibilities (see Figure 9.3). Public safety is the biggest expenditure for California cities, whereas welfare is the biggest county expenditure.

Budget Woes

Although Proposition 13 is much loved by homeowners for reducing property tax bills, the initiative caused serious fiscal problems for local governments by cutting property tax revenues and making approval of new taxes or tax increases more difficult. That combination necessitated severe budget cuts for cities and counties. Beyond that, Proposition 13 gave the state the responsibility to allocate property taxes among local governments even as Proposition 98 (see Chapter 8) mandated allocation of a fixed percentage of the state budget to education. As a consequence, a portion of property taxes that had previously gone to cities and counties was shifted to schools—putting even further pressure on city and county budgets and resulting in further cuts in services. Moreover, cities and counties, which previously had some control of their own revenues, became dependent on the state for property and sales tax revenues, a significant loss of local control.[8]

These problems have been compounded by recessions in the early 1990s and again in 2001–2003 and 2009–2010 followed by a very slow recovery. Parts of the state were hit hard by foreclosures on home loans, property values fell across the state, and property tax revenues for local governments fell—along with sales tax revenues. Other factors exacerbated the crisis for local governments.

In 2004 Governor Arnold Schwarzenegger exacerbated circumstances for local governments by drastically reducing vehicle license fees, which had previously been a significant source of local revenues. In 2009, facing a continued deficit, the state resorted—not for the first time—to a massive "take-back" of local property tax revenues, diverting nearly $4 billion in local property taxes from schools, cities, counties, and redevelopment agencies. Then in 2011,

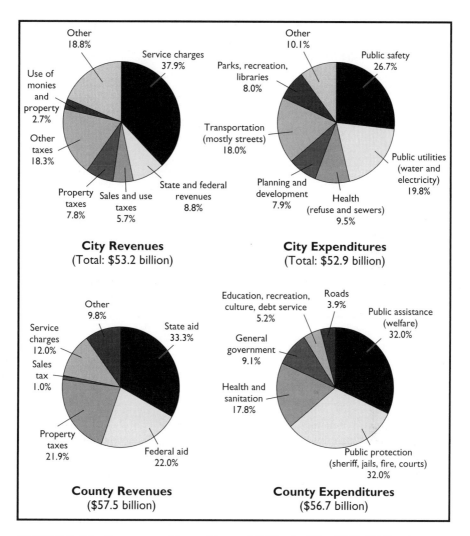

City Revenues
(Total: $53.2 billion)

City Expenditures
(Total: $52.9 billion)

County Revenues
($57.5 billion)

County Expenditures
($56.7 billion)

F I G U R E 9.3 Revenues and Expenditures of California Cities (2009–2010) and Counties (2010–2011)

SOURCE: California State Controller, 2012, http://www.sco.ca.gov.

Governor Brown abolished local redevelopment agencies—governmental entities created by cities to fund new development in declining areas—and transferred most of their $5 billion in annual revenues to schools and other state services.

Frustrated by all this, cities and counties pushed back with ballot measures to prevent state take-backs and transfers and guarantee future revenues. Voters approved propositions designed to do this in 2004 and 2010, and the state is now somewhat more constrained. Take-backs can still occur, but the state must eventually repay the funds. Nevertheless, in the short term the take-backs only worsened the fiscal problems of local governments. Cities also challenged the state's elimination of redevelopment agencies, but the courts ruled that since the state had created the agencies, the state had the authority to do away with them. Meanwhile, counties worried the state would not provide adequate compensation for the costs of moving nonviolent felons from prisons to county jails (Governor Brown's "realignment").

All of this has driven many California cities and counties to the fiscal brink. Oakland and other cities have laid off hundreds of police officers, despite rising crime rates. Los Angeles mayor Antonio Villaraigoso, usually an ally of public employees, proposed layoffs and demanded salary concessions from the city's unions. Maywood, in Southern California, laid off all its city employees, including police officers, and contracted with other cities for some services and with Los Angeles County for police protection. "We will become 100 percent a contracted city," said Maywood's interim city manager.[9] Other cities also considered contracting for services. San Jose has "outsourced" graffiti abatement and some maintenance work. Redding, in Northern California, and Santa Clarita, in Southern California, have contracted with a private company to provide library services. Still other cities considered merging police or fire departments with neighboring cities. In some areas, reformers called for consolidation of small school districts, special districts, and cities as a partial solution to budget problems.

Many cities and other local agencies also face fiscal strain due to the pensions and other benefits they offered their employees when their budgets were flush with cash. Now unable to meet these commitments but bound by contracts, local governments have sought to renegotiate contracts to win concessions from current employees or to move to a two-tier pension system, preserving benefits for current workers but reducing them for future hires. Voters in Modesto, Palo Alto, San Diego, San Francisco, and San Jose have overwhelmingly approved pension reform, but the problem persists and pensions take up an ever-growing portion of local budgets—money that might otherwise fund police, libraries, and other local services.

More drastically, some cities, including Vallejo (near San Francisco) in 2008 and Mammoth Lakes, San Bernardino, and Stockton in 2012, have declared bankruptcy. Unable to pay employee salaries or repay bonded indebtedness, bankruptcy allowed these cities to legally suspend payments and renegotiate contracts while a bankruptcy judge determines which creditors should be paid. In all cases, city services, including public safety, were cut drastically. Unique circumstances in each of these cities contributed to their dire straits, but some observers worried that bankruptcies would spread to other California cities.

LOCAL GOVERNMENT IN PERSPECTIVE

Despite their fiscal trials, local governments remain a major component of the California economy, with nearly 1.5 million employees (half are in education) and combined budgets totaling over $207 billion. Local governments cost a lot, but they also do a lot.

Yet, as demonstrated by Proposition 13, realignment, and ongoing budget battles, the state limits what local governments can do. Some may dispute such interventions, but the state's authority remains supreme. Nevertheless, opinion polls consistently report that Californians view local government more favorably than state government. Whatever its limitations, California's political system gives residents many opportunities to decide what sort of communities they want, and many Californians take advantage of these opportunities by engaging in local politics.

NOTES

1. Zoltan L. Hajnal, Paul G. Lewis, and Hugh Louch, "Municipal Elections in California: Turnout, Timing, and Competition," Public Policy Institute of California, March 2002.

2. Jessica Trounstine and Zoltan Hajnal, "Low Voter Turnout Does Matter: Spending Priorities in Local Politics" (paper presented at the annual meeting of the Midwest Political Science Association, Chicago, April 2004).

3. Hajnal, Lewis, and Louch, *op. cit.*

4. EdSource, www.edsource.org (accessed August 21, 2012).

5. *Ibid.* (accessed August 22, 2012) or see California Budget Project, "School Finance Facts," October 2011, www.cbp.org (accessed August 22, 2012).

6. For more on regional fragmentation and special districts, see Brian, P. Janiskee, "The Problem of Local Government in California," in *California Republic*, ed. Brian P. Janiskee and Ken Masugi (Lanham, Md.: Rowman and Littlefield, 2004).

7. California Elections Data Archive, Institute for Social Research, California State University, Sacramento, www.csus.edu/isr (accessed August 22, 2012).

8. For further discussion of these effects of Proposition 13, see John Decker, *California in the Balance* (Berkeley, Calif.: Berkeley Public Policy Press, 2009), pp. xi, 116, 137–138.

9. "Maywood to Lay Off All City Employees, Dismantle Police Department," June 22, 2010, www.latimesblogs.latimes.com/lanow/2010/06.

LEARN MORE ON THE WEB

ABZY News Links (listing state and local media and online news sources):
www.abyznewslinks.com/uniteca.htm

California Elections Data Archive (CEDA) (information on local elections):
www.csus.edu/isr/reports/california_elections/index.html

California State Association of Counties:
www.csac.counties.org

California State Controller (data on cities, counties, schools, and special districts): www.sco.ca.gov

On instant runoff voting (IRV): www.instantrunoff.com

League of California Cities: www.cacities.org

Public Policy Institute of California (studies on local government): www.ppic.org

LEARN MORE AT THE LIBRARY

Terry Christensen and Tom Hogen-Esch. *Local Politics: A Practical Guide to Governing at the Grassroots*. Armonk, N.Y.: M. E. Sharpe, 2006.

Jack Citrin and Isaac William Martin, eds. *After the Tax Revolt: California's Proposition 13 Turns 30*. Berkeley: Institute of Government Studies, 2009.

Paul G. Lewis. *Deep Roots: Local Government Structure in California*. San Francisco: Public Policy Institute of California, 1998.

GET INVOLVED

Contact your city's mayor or a member of your city council or county board of supervisors to volunteer or to apply for an internship. Go to your city or county's Web site to find the elected officials. You can also intern with a community group—just search for one that interests you on the Internet.

10

✳

State-Federal Relations: Conflict, Cooperation, and Chaos

CHAPTER CONTENTS

California's uniqueness stems in part from its position as the nation's most populated state; it also emanates from the state's vast resources, size, diversity, and engagement in thorny issues. We see problems and their outcomes on a scale here unequaled elsewhere. And so it is with the state's relationship with the federal government, which can be described as wary, uneven, and often fraught with controversy.

Sometimes state and national leaders differ over California's management. Public education reform is one such policy area, with the federal government and state legislature at odds over the definition of *reform*. On other issues, such as water policy, however, the two governments have worked well together. There are also instances where California has acted with its own response to

135

national issues, with the federal government eventually moving into line; nowhere is this more obvious than with environmental protection. Deciding the best responses to problems that affect both the nation and state can be a challenge because, like its forty-nine counterparts, California is both a self-governing entity and a member of the larger national government.

Matters become even more complicated when determining financial responsibility for costly issues such as massive transportation projects, immigration control, or health-care policy, to name a few. Because the state is so large and complex, federal assistance almost always seems inadequate. When federal aid or programs are cut, California seems to suffer disproportionately compared with other states.

Nevertheless, when the state confronts a complex issue, its struggle is often the precursor of similar concerns likely to affect the rest of the nation. The women's right-to-choose movement, gun control, the tax revolt, medical marijuana, stem cell research, and same-sex marriage all had early beginnings, and in some cases, origins—in California.

In this chapter we review California's impact on national policymaking and policy actors. We also explore some of the critical policy areas that test California's relationship with the federal government: immigration, greenhouse gas emissions, and the distribution of federal resources to the state of California. Each topic touches on the delicate balance between state autonomy and national objectives—perspectives in federalism that are not always viewed the same ways by state and federal government leaders.

CALIFORNIA'S CLOUT WITH THE PRESIDENT

Despite its size and huge bloc of Electoral College votes, California hasn't figured prominently in presidential elections in recent years, largely because the state has been predictably secure for Democratic candidates on every occasion since 1992. As a consequence, we don't see the candidates as much as voters do in other states. Republican presidential candidates do not invest significant resources on California because they don't see much return, and Democrats stay away because of their need to pursue electoral votes in more competitive states. But California is important to both national political parties in one major respect, namely, as the top state for campaign contributions. That alone keeps candidates coming to places such as Orange County, Silicon Valley, and Hollywood.

California has had an uneven relationship with the nation's presidents. For example, Republican President George W. Bush was not particularly helpful to the state largely due to his general hands-off attitude on domestic policy issues. When then-Governor Gray Davis demanded federal prosecution of big power companies for a price-fixing scheme that caused an energy crisis in 2001, the Bush administration refused, although the courts eventually found otherwise. Other areas of disinterest on the president's part included agriculture, border patrol assistance, and terrorism funding. Given the clash of cultural and political values between most Californians and the conservative Republican president, it's easy to see why the distance between the state and the president was more than a matter of miles.

President Barack Obama has been somewhat more responsive to California's issues, particularly on questions relating to government support for "green" technology research and production. The Obama administration has also embraced California's strict rules on automobile exhaust emissions, a departure from the approach of George W. Bush. On transportation, Obama has funneled federal funds for the state's massive high-speed rail project, although California's recent budget problems have led many to question the wisdom of the $69 billion effort, even with federal dollars. Still, not everything has gone California's way. The Obama administration compensated California for only a fraction of the hundreds of millions of dollars spent by the state on incarcerate of illegal immigrants awaiting deportation to their home countries. And California has wrested very little of Obama's "Race to the Top" education improvement funds at a time when public education has been gasping for support. Still, on balance, California has had more success with President Obama than his predecessor.

CALIFORNIA'S CLOUT WITH CONGRESS

As the nation's most populated state, California has fifty-three members in the House of Representatives, dwarfing the delegations of every other state. Texas and New York are second and third, with thirty-two and twenty-nine members, respectively. The majority party in each house of Congress chooses committee chairs who, in turn, control the flow of national legislation.

The twenty-first century began with Republicans enjoying control of both houses. In 2006 growing discontent with the war in Iraq, an uneven national economy, and political corruption in Congress led the nation's voters to elect a Democratic majority to the House of Representatives. San Francisco's Nancy Pelosi, elected in 2002 to the post of minority leader, was elected Speaker. With that elevation, she assumed the highest national leadership post ever held in the United States by a woman. As a result of the election outcome, several prominent California Democrats assumed key committee chairmanships by virtue of their years of seniority in the House.

Political party fortunes turned in 2010 when the Republicans captured control of the House, resulting in four committee chairmanships for California Republicans: Oversight and Governmental Reform (Darrell Issa); Armed Services (Howard "Buck" McKeon; House Administration (Dan Lungren); and Rules (David Dreier). In addition, Kevin McCarthy was elected majority whip, the third highest party post after Speaker and majority leader. Republicans retained control of the House after the 2012 election.

The political winds also have shifted in the U.S. Senate, but not as much as in the House. Although the upper house is a bit less partisan than the lower house, the majority party still controls all committee chairmanships, and therefore the flow of legislation. In 2006 the off-year revolution produced a slim 51-to-49 Democratic majority, thanks to two independents who promised their loyalty to the Democratic side of the aisle. Suddenly, Senators Dianne Feinstein and Barbara Boxer, both first elected in 1992, emerged as key players on issues dealing with the environment, foreign relations, and the judiciary. By 2009 the Democratic majority hit 60, a number large enough to cut off filibusters. Since then, the Democratic majority has narrowed considerably. Still, California Democrats retain clout. Boxer, reelected in 2010, chairs the Environment and Public Works Committee and the Senate Select Committee on Ethics. Feinstein, reelected in 2012, chairs the Senate Select Committee on Intelligence.

Democrats in California enjoy a comfortable margin of 38–15 over Republicans in the House of Representatives. In other respects California's congressional makeup is as diverse as the rest of the state. As of 2013, the delegation includes 9 Latinos, 3 African-Americans, 5 Asian-Americans, 18 women and 1 gay member. Both of California's U.S. senators are women as well.

Divisiveness

One other fact must be added to the discussion of Californians in Washington: historically, California's **congressional delegation** has been notoriously fractured on key public policy issues affecting California. Much of the conflict stems from the state's complexity. North/south, urban/suburban/rural, and coastal/valley/mountain divisions separate the state geographically. Other differences exist, too, in terms of wealth, ethnicity, and basic liberal/conservative distinctions. To be sure, no congressional district is completely homogeneous, yet most members of Congress tend to protect their districts' interests more than those of the state as a whole. Thus, on issues ranging from desert protection to immigration reform, California's representatives have often canceled each other's votes, leaving states such as Texas far more powerful because of their relatively unified stances. Even on foreign trade, members from California often have worked at cross-purposes, depending on the industries, interest groups, and demographic characteristics of their districts.

Only on the question of offshore oil drilling have most members of the state's delegation voted the same way. In 2008, with gasoline prices hitting record levels, President George W. Bush called for an end to the twenty-seven–year federal moratorium on offshore drilling. Almost the entire California delegation opposed the proposal, and the damaging Gulf of Mexico offshore oil blowout in 2010 silenced any further discussion.

Controversy over the Proposed Auburn Dam—Case in Point

The struggle over the proposed Auburn Dam in Northern California is a current case in point. California hungers for more water, but the real debate has been over the best ways to get it and at what cost. The massive $9.6 billion proposal has been considered in Congress since 1960. Federal agencies have spent $325 million just on feasibility studies. Yet California lawmakers in Washington have remained paralyzed over the issue, largely due to the conflicting objectives of environmentalists and farmers. The various sides struck a compromise in 2003 by upgrading another dam downstream. But concerns over California's weakened levee system led House Republican Dan Lungren to pursue the idea yet again in 2007 after the release of a 152-page report by the U.S. Department of the Interior.[1] Meanwhile, Democrats Pete Stark and George Miller have used their clout to thwart consideration of the project as an environmentally unsound proposal. Ironically, both Stark and Lungren lost their seats in the 2012 election. The issue of whether the project is a boondoggle or a vital flood-control program is not as significant as the fact that it has polarized the California congressional delegation. Meanwhile, as Californians have fussed among themselves over this vexing question, representatives from other states have worked in bipartisan ways to garner federal dollars for their projects.

HIGH-SPEED RAIL

In 2008, California voters passed **Proposition 1A**, which committed the state $9.95 billion in bonds to partially fund an 800-mile long high-speed rail program. Officially known as the Safe, Reliable High-Speed Passenger Train Bond Act for the 21st Century, the ballot proposition was the down payment of a transportation system projected to cost $43 billion. Proponents touted the rail network as an environmentally friendly enterprise equivalent to the addition of twelve polluting highway lanes up and down the length of the state.

The new Obama administration gushed over the transportation network as a twenty-first century infrastructure gem and immediately made available $3.3 billion in matching federal funds for the first segment of construction, which federal transportation officials required on the 130-mile stretch between Chowchilla and Bakersfield. The money would be available as long as the state committed to the project no later than September 2012. In July 2012, the legislature voted to spend $2.7 billion of the 2008 bond for the first leg of construction.

Meanwhile, critics began to question the legitimacy of the high-speed rail project. The Great Recession hit California even harder than most states, causing state budget revenues to tank. Every year between 2008 and 2012, state leaders had to find ways to overcome annual deficits of $20 billion or more. Technically, the state budget was separate from the High-Speed Rail Bonds, but few Californians made that distinction. In addition, the transportation project suffered a double-whammy through a new estimated cost of $99 billion and projections of fewer riders.[2] At the same time, leaders in the now Republican-led House of Representatives balked at providing federal funds. Ironically, the opposition effort was led by two Californians, Central Valley-based Jeff Denham, who voted for the project earlier as a state legislator, and Kevin McCarthy, the House majority whip from Bakersfield.[3]

In 2012, the High-Speed Rail Commission, the project's governing authority, produced a revised plan which cut the cost of the transportation system to $68 billion over about 520 miles of track. But that did little to assuage the growing number of opponents. The nonpartisan Legislative Analyst's Office urged lawmakers to end the project. Public opinion polls found the voters now wanting to vote again on the idea, with sizable numbers against it. Still, Governor Jerry Brown remained supportive of the project "without any hesitation."[4] Proponents added that new state funds would come from the state's cap-and-trade pollution revenues beginning in 2014, with the continued implementation of California's AB32, the state's Global Warming Solutions Act.

Countless questions remain about the High-Speed Rail program. Will the federal government continue to provide funding in a tie of great austerity? Will the state generate enough funds to pay for the railroad? If constructed, will the new transportation network fulfill expectations? For the moment, the outcome of this story remains a mystery.

IMMIGRATION

California has long been a magnet for those in search of opportunity. And they have come—first the Spanish; then Yankee, Irish, and Chinese immigrants during the nineteenth century; followed by Japanese, Eastern European, African American, and Vietnamese immigrants beginning in the 1970s, Asian Indians in the 1990s, and more Latinos throughout the last half century (see Table 10.1). But over the past two decades, several factors have converged to influence the moods of the state's residents and would-be residents. Lack of opportunity in other nations has led millions to choose California as an alternative; meanwhile, an overburdened and underfunded infrastructure has led many of those already here to oppose further immigration. Much of the antipathy has been directed at

T A B L E 10.1 California's Immigrants: Leading Countries of Origin, 2009

Country	Number
Mexico	4,308,000
Philippines	783,000
China (incl. Taiwan)	681,000
Vietnam	457,000
El Salvador	413,000
India	319,000
Korea	307,000
Guatemala	261,000
Iran	214,000
Canada	132,000
United Kingdom	125,000
Japan	105,000

SOURCE: U.S. Decennial Census, 2009.

Latinos—particularly those from Mexico—but anger has also been aimed at Asians.

The numbers are substantial. Whereas 15.1 percent of California's population were foreign born in 1980, 27.2 percent fell within that category in 2010, with projections showing that percentage remaining in place through 2030.[5] During the same period, the percentage of foreign-born residents of the United States as a whole nearly doubled to 12.1 percent from 6.2 percent (see Figure 10.1). Between 1990 and 2005, more than 40 percent of California's population growth came from foreign immigration. In 2010 the Pew Hispanic Center estimated that there were between 11.4 million and 12.4 million illegal immigrants nationwide, with between 2.5 million and 2.85 million of them in California.[6] Still, the percentage of illegal immigrants living in California dropped from 42 percent to 22 percent, indicating greater movement elsewhere.[7]

With these dramatic events reshaping California, experts have argued about whether the immigrants help or harm the state's economy. One recent study finds that only about one-third of recent immigrants have health insurance, suggesting a financial burden for public health institutions and services.[8] Yet other studies show that immigrants, legal and illegal combined, are very similar in economic makeup to the rest of America.[9] Moreover, illegal immigrants are critical to some industries such as California farming, where they make up as much

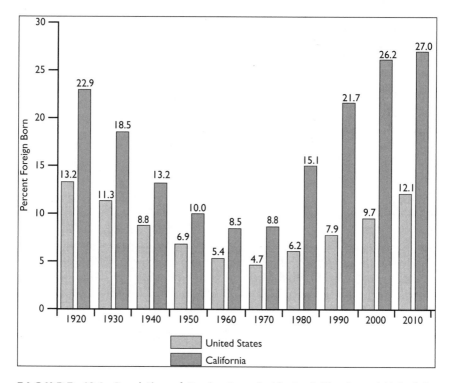

FIGURE 10.1 Population of Foreign-Born Residents, California and United States Comparison

as 90 percent of the harvest workforce. To the extent that these workers are excluded from the fields, California's $40 billion agriculture industry could suffer irreparable damage.[10] All these findings suggest a growing ambivalence toward the illegal immigration issue in California.

None of this has stopped the federal government from moving on immigration, although not always with consistency. In 2008 the Bush administration increased surveillance of U.S. companies with illegal immigrant employees, leading to fines for employers, deportation for undocumented workers, and workforce shortages. Between a more vigilant border protection system and a declining U.S. economy, the number of attempted border crossings by illegal immigrants declined. That, and a weak American economy, led more than 1 million illegal immigrants to return to their home countries by 2010.[11]

The largest issue related to immigration is determining which level of government should assume responsibility for its costs. While the federal government has long established the criteria for immigration and the conditions for enforcement, it leaves the states responsible for meeting the needs of immigrants. Nowhere does this contradiction ring louder than in California. Among unauthorized immigrants alone, recent estimates cite health-care costs of $1.5 billion, education costs for 923,000 of their children at $4 billion, and incarceration costs for 19,000 illegal immigrants at $970 million.[12] Few of these costs have been completely absorbed by the federal government, yet their day-to-day impact is a reality.

Controversy continues over the illegal immigration issue. Since his election, President Obama repeatedly has pushed Congress for immigration reform that would allow citizenship after a multi-year period of residence, assuming law-abiding behavior by illegal immigrants. The Republican-led majority in the House of Representatives has resisted the proposal, leaving individual states to wrestle with the issue. Clearly, the role of each government in managing the immigration question remains a tough issue to sort out. President Obama added to the drama in 2012 when he signed an executive order allowing as many as 800,000 young illegal immigrants to remain in the United States under specific conditions.[13]

CLIMATE CHANGE

California and the federal government have had a rocky relationship with respect to climate change. At times, the state has fought national objectives; at others, California has taken the lead. So it is with the issue of air quality. According to the U.S. **Environmental Protection Agency (EPA)**, the ten smoggiest counties in the nation are found in California. Metropolitan Los Angeles, an area that extends east to Riverside and south to Long Beach, tops the list as the smoggiest area in the nation. Actually, the number of "unhealthful" days in the L.A. basin declined from an average of 189.6 during the 1996–1998 period to 141.8 between 2006 and 2008, according to the American Lung Association, although progress has slowed since 2004.[14] Statewide, the costs have been great. One recent study finds that annual losses in California from unhealthy air amount to $28 billion in the form of premature deaths, illness, and lost productivity in the workplace.[15]

Congress and the EPA have been unhappy with the inability of the state to move forward on clean air. But given the state's dependence on manufacturing, particularly in the vast Los Angeles basin, it has been difficult to meet national standards without choking off the local economy. In 1992 state regulators established the Regional Clean Air Incentives Market Program (RECLAIM) in Southern California, a program in which manufacturers buy and sell emissions permits as a means of encouraging emissions reduction. The program has led to substantial reductions in environmental decay, although the region remains far from healthy.

Automobile exhaust is another story, however. California has led the nation in reducing auto emissions which account for 28 percent of the state's greenhouse gases. Since the passage of the federal Clean Air Act of 1970, state environmental regulators have asked for and received forty-four waivers from the EPA to establish standards beyond federal requirements. That's what happened routinely until 2007, when the Bush administration's EPA rejected the claim that auto emissions contained greenhouse gases, to the amazement of most scientists in the United States and worldwide.[16] Since the agency gave no scientific explanation for its ruling, California and sixteen other states sued the EPA for not carrying out its mandate. The United States Supreme Court agreed.

The political environment regarding auto emissions changed dramatically with the election of Barack Obama to the presidency in 2008. Early in 2009 he asked his new EPA administrator to review previous decisions on California's waiver petitions. In June 2009 the agency approved California's proposal and announced a new national policy on higher gasoline mileage and lower emissions by 2017, based on California's standards. On this occasion, at least, California set the trend for the rest of the nation.

WATER

Not all of California's jurisdictional disputes have occurred with the federal government. On the issue of water, California repeatedly has tangled with other states. Simply put, the state doesn't have enough. Three-quarters of California's water comes from north of Sacramento, while 80 percent is consumed south of Sacramento. Most of the imbalance is corrected through two giant transfer systems. The federal Central Valley Project, which dates from 1937, supplies the farmers of the southern Central Valley. The State Water Project, begun in 1960, largely supplies southern urban areas. Both systems intercept freshwater near the Sacramento–San Joaquin Delta before it can flow out to the ocean. Still, California gasps for more water, which has led to confrontations with other states.

The linchpin of the water frenzy among western states is the Colorado River, the freshwater source that begins in Colorado and empties into the Gulf of California. Under a 1922 multistate agreement, California is entitled to 4.4 million acre-feet, or 59 percent, of the lower basin river annually. Yet according to some critics, California exceeded its share by as much as 800,000 acre-feet per year, enough to provide for the annual water needs of 1.6 million households in rapidly growing Arizona and Nevada.[17]

Fearing a bruising battle that would spill into Congress, officials from seven states held talks for eighteen months to resolve the problem. In 2000 they agreed to a formula that would allow California to gradually reduce its consumption of the excess over a fifteen-year period. But the end date for that agreement is fast approaching, and it remains to be seen what, if any new arrangement will follow. At least for the time being, the seven western states have solved a troublesome issue without federal participation.

Meanwhile, the federal government's Department of the Interior and the state of California quieted the ongoing three-way battle among agribusiness (which consumes 80 percent of the state's water), environmentalists seeking to preserve rivers and deltas, and urban areas in need of water to grow. The two governments developed a plan in 2000 to expand existing federal reservoirs in California, improve drinking water quality, and develop a creative water recycling program. Most of the $8.5 billion price tag has been shouldered by the federal government, with Californians providing $825 million. In 2004 Congress committed another $10 billion over thirty years to improve the quality of water flowing into the Sacramento Delta and San Francisco Bay.

Uncertainties remain, however. In 2002 the U.S. Department of the Interior modified a plan previously favored by environmentalists by directing more water from the Central Valley Project to farmers, rather than using it for ecosystem restoration. Still, water can be distributed to customers only if it is available, and recent droughts in California and the West have left the region thirsty. For example, in 2007, a record-low snowpack in the Sierra Nevada Mountains and concern for endangered species led a federal court judge to reduce deliveries of Northern California water to Southern California by 25 percent, imperiling agriculture and construction projects alike.[18]

In 2012, Governor Jerry Brown laid out plans to divert additional water from the Sacramento Delta in an effort to meet the state's growing needs. No sooner than the governor delivered his announcement, several members of the California congressional delegation registered concerns with U.S. Secretary of the Interior Ken Salazar about southern California interests "who would steal our water."[19] So the struggle over water continues, both between California and the federal government and also between farmers, environmentalists, and developers.

SHARED RESOURCES

"Federalism" refers to the multifaceted political relationship that binds the state and national governments. One aspect centers on financial assistance that wends its way from federal coffers to state and local treasuries, and that amounted to about $567 billion in fiscal year 2013, down from $625 billion in fiscal year 2011. Most of this assistance comes in the form of **grants-in-aid**, amounting to about 20 percent of all state and local government revenues. The money flows through more than six hundred federal programs covering areas from agricultural development to high-tech research.

For decades, California received more than its fair share of grants-in-aid from the federal government. That has changed. In 1983 California had 10 percent of the national population but received 22 percent of the national government's expenditures, thanks largely to defense- and space-related research. Then came the slide. With a pared defense budget, cutbacks in infrastructure work, and the push for a balanced budget, federal contributions have shrunk considerably over the past two decades. As of 2010 California had 11.9 percent of the nation's population but received 10.8 percent of the nation's federal funds. The state now ranks forty-fourth in the distribution of federal spending on a per capita basis-down sharply from twentieth in 1990.[20]

There is another way to appreciate the changing relationship between the federal government and California. Because of the state's massive growth, California had a long history of getting more dollars from the federal government than it contributed. Beginning in 1986, however, California became a "donor" state. Ever since, California has contributed more money to the national treasury than it has received, and the disparity is increasing every year. In 1992, for every dollar California sent to Washington, D.C., the state received 93 cents in federal goods and services. By 2005, for every dollar California sent to Washington, only 78 cents came back in goods and services (see Table 10.2). Even when California and the rest of the states received a larger federal commitment from the Economic Stimulus Act in 2009 and 2010, the state's share ranked in the bottom half of the per capita federal expenditures. No matter how you slice it, California is getting less of the federal "pie" today than in the past.

T A B L E 10.2 Federal Expenditures per Dollar of Taxes, Fiscal Years 1992 and 2010—California and Selected States

	Expenditures per Dollar of Taxes		Ranking	
	FY1992	FY2010	FY1992	FY2010
New Mexico	$2.08	$2.05	11	4
California	$.93	$1.09	38	27 (t)*
Kansas	$1.05	$1.04	27	29
Texas	$.93	$.91	37	41 (t)*
Maryland	$1.27	$.86	15	44
Massachusetts	$1.01	$.83	31	46
New Jersey	$.66	$.77	50	48

*t means tied with another state.

SOURCES: Tax Foundation, Bureau of Economic Analysis, Internal Revenue Service.

But there is more to the story than just dollars in and dollars out; it's what the dollars buy that makes a huge difference, and in California the high cost of living makes national numbers meaningless. Data compiled in 2011 by California Watch, an independent research organization, found that a family of four in this state needs about $63,000 per year to cover basic needs; that's nearly triple the federal level.[21] And when we consider that the state's immigrant population is more than twice the national average on a per capita basis, it becomes clear that the state's needs fare particularly poorly when it comes to federal funding.

California fared slightly better with the distribution of funds from the American Recovery and Reinvestment Act in 2009 and 2010, when Congress passed an $831 billion bill to help pull the nation out of the worst recession since the Great Depression. On a per capita basis, California ranked twenty-ninth in federal payments. However, at the same time, the state's unemployment was the third highest in the nation.[22] It's important to remember that although the state gained a larger share of federal funds because of the economic crisis, those dollars stopped coming in 2011.

The data presented here counter the political posturing that has emerged from both Congress and the presidency in recent years. They reveal a state that has given much more to the federal government in taxes than it has received in programs and services. They also reflect the fragmentation that has haunted the state's congressional delegation. As a result, California's "Golden State" nickname has a different meaning in Washington than in California—namely, sizable economic resources that have landed disproportionately in the federal treasury.

CALIFORNIA TODAY: GOLDEN STATE
OR FOOL'S GOLD?

Is today's California still the state with unlimited potential or the state with too many burdens to survive? When it comes to relations with the federal government, perhaps the answer is a little of both. California is king when it comes to campaign contributions for national candidates, research and development, the center of agriculture, and auto emissions standards. At the same time, California is a pauper in matters of dealing with a perpetual state budget deficit, a dilapidated infrastructure, and a frayed social safety net. Once upon a time, the state would have looked to the federal government for rescue, and the federal government might have provided some relief. That relationship has been replaced by one in which the two governments are often at odds.

As noted at the beginning of this chapter, some of the shift has been because of the ebb and flow of national politics. Thus, during the Clinton years, the state benefited from extra federal attention on research and development tax credits, H1-B visas for skilled workers, and even some defense contracts. During the Bush years, California didn't fare so well, as attested by the administration's disregard for the state's immigration issues, water management, and exorbitant electricity bills.

Under President Obama, California has received support for continuation of the research and development tax credit, high-speed rail, and assistance for

California homeowners dealing with foreclosure issues. At the same time, federal dollars for public education and recovery from the Great Recession have been relatively sparse. Whether Obama's second term provides more financial support for California remains to be seen.

If nothing else, California operates with more financial autonomy from the federal government today than in the times of heavy government defense spending. To this extent the state has experienced a reduced federal reliance, although the state's woefully unbalanced annual budget surely would benefit from more federal support. Accordingly, California's growing fiscal self-reliance may be the hallmark of the state's direction in the coming years. Whatever the future, it will be an interesting experiment.

NOTES

1. U.S. Department of Interior, "Reclamation: Managing Water in the West, Auburn-Folsom South Unit Special Report," December 2006.

2. "Forecast Dire for Riders, Revenue," *San Jose Mercury News*, October 11, 2011, pp. A1, A8.

3. "Bullet Train Funds in GOP Sights," *Los Angeles Times*, October 23, 2011, pp. AA1, AA4.

4. "Jerry Brown Defends High-Speed Rail," *San Francisco Chronicle*, January 19, 2012, p. A1.

5. U.S. Census Bureau, http//quickfacts.census.gov/qfd/states/06000.html (accessed July 27, 2012).

6. Jeffrey Passel and D'Vera Cohn, "Unauthorized Immigrant Population: National and State Trends, 2010," Pew Hispanic Center, 2011, www.pewhispanic.org (accessed August 31, 2012).

7. "Illegal Immigrants Become Subject of Coverage Debate," *San Francisco Chronicle*, September 11, 2009, pp. A1, A18.

8. *The Size and Characteristics of the Unauthorized Migrant Population in the U.S.* (Washington, D.C.: Pew Hispanic Center, 2006), pp. A1, A18.

9. "Immigrants in the Work Force: Study Belies Image," *The New York Times*, April 10, 2010, pp. A1, A3.

10. "Farmers Oppose G.O.P. Bill to Require Verification of Workers' Immigration Status," *The New York Times*, July 31, 2011, pp. A12, A16.

11. "Number of Illegal Immigrants from Mexico Drops," http://www.azcentral.com/news/politics/articles/2012/04/23/20120423illegal-immgrant-population-study-mexico-united-states.html, April 23, 3012.

12. "Illegal Immigrants Are a Factor in the Budget Map Gap," *Los Angeles Times*, February 2, 2009, http://articles.latimes.com/2009/feb/02/local/me-cap2.

13. According to The *New York Times*, the U.S. government "will no longer initiate the deportation of illegal immigrants who came to the United States before age 16, have lived here for at least five years, and are in school, are high school graduates or are military veterans in good standing. The immigrants must also be not more than

30 years old and have clean criminal records." "Obama to Permit Young Migrants to Remain in the United States," *The New York Times*, http://www.nytimes.com/2012/06/16/us/us-to-stop-deporting-some-illegal-immigrants.html?pagewanted=all.

14. "Smog in L.A. Still Tops in Nation," *Los Angeles Times*, April 28, 2010, pp. AA1, AA6.

15. Daniel A. Mazmanian, "Achieving Air Quality: The Los Angeles Experience" (unpublished paper,) University of Southern California, March 2006, p. 28.

16. "E.P.A. Says 17 States Can't Set Greenhouse Gas Rules for Cars," The *New York Times*, December 20, 2007, pp. A1, A30.

17. "California Water Users Miss Deadline for Pact Sharing," The *New York Times*, January 1, 2003. The six states in addition to California are Arizona, Colorado, Nevada, New Mexico, Utah, and Wyoming.

18. "Enforcing Recent Water Laws May Throttle State's Growth," *Los Angeles Times*, January 14, 2008, pp. B1, B8.

19. "California Members of Congress Demand That the Bay Delta Conservation Plan Be Fair and Equitable," YubaNet.com, http://yubanet.com/california/California-Members-of-Congress-Demand-that-the-Bay-Delta-Conservation-Plan-Be-Fair-and-Equitable_printer.php, (accessed May 17, 2012).

20. U.S. Census, Consolidated Federal Funds Report for Fiscal Year 2010, September 2011, http//www.census.gov/prod/2011pubs/effr-10pdf (accessed August 31, 2012).

21. "Federal Poverty Level Doesn't Meet Basic Needs, Data Shows," *California Watch*, October 11, 2011, http//californiawatch.org/print/12903 (accessed August 31, 2012).

22. "Stimulus Benefits and Unemployment," *USA Today*, August 4, 2010, p. 5A.

LEARN MORE ON THE WEB

California and federal taxes:
www.taxfoundation.org

Californi Institute for Federal Policy Research:
www.calinst.org

Environmental Protection Agency:
www.epa.gov

Immigration:
www.irps.ucsd.edu

Office of Management and Budget:
www.whitehouse.gov/omb

U.S. House of Representatives:
www.house.gov

U.S. Senate:
www.senate.gov

LEARN MORE AT THE LIBRARY

Larry N. Gerston. *American Federalism: A Concise Introduction*. Armonk, N.Y.: M. E. Sharpe, 2007.

Laurence J. O'Toole. *American Intergovernmental Relations: Foundations, Perspectives, and Issues*. 4th ed. Washington, D.C.: CQ Press, 2007.

David Brian Robertson, *Federalism and the Making of America*. New York, Routledge, 2012.

G. Ross Stephens and Nelson Wikstrom. *American Intergovernmental Relations: A Fragmented Federal Polity*. New York: Oxford University Press, 2007.

GET INVOLVED

Contact your congress member to volunteer or apply for an internship in his or her district office. To find your representative, go to: www.house.gov /representatives/find/.

Glossary

at-large elections City council elections in which all candidates are elected by the community as a whole rather than by districts.

attorney general The elected top law enforcement officer and legal counsel; the second most powerful member of the executive branch.

bank and corporation tax A tax on the profits of lending institutions and businesses; the third most important source of state revenue.

bicameral legislature Organization of the state legislature into two houses: the forty-member senate (elected for four-year terms) and the eighty-member assembly (elected for two-year terms).

Big Five The governor, assembly speaker, assembly minority leader, senate president pro tem, and senate minority leader, who gather together informally to thrash out decisions on the annual budget and other major policy issues.

Board of Equalization The five-member state board that maintains uniform property tax assessments and oversees the collection of sales, gasoline, and liquor taxes; members are elected by district; part of the executive branch.

board of supervisors The five-member governing body of counties; elected by district to four-year terms.

bonds Subject to voter approval, state and local governments can borrow money by issuing bonds, which are repaid (with interest) from the general fund budget or from special taxes or fees.

bureaucracy State or local government workers employed through the civil service system rather than appointed by the governor or other elected officials.

central committees Political party organizations at county and state levels; weakly linked to one another.

charges for services Local government fees for services such as sewage treatment, trash collection, building permits, and the use of recreational facilities; a major source of income for cities and counties since the passage of Proposition 13 in 1978.

charter The equivalent of a constitution for a local government; includes government structures, election systems, powers of officeholders, conditions for employing local government workers, and often much more.

charter city or county A local government that drafts its own structures and organization through a document like a local constitution (also known as a "home-rule" charter), subject to voter approval.

cities Local governments in urban areas, run by city councils and mayors or city managers; principal responsibilities include police and fire protection, land use planning, street maintenance and construction, sanitation, libraries, and parks.

Citizens Redistricting Commission Enacted by the voters in Proposition 11 (2008), this commission is responsible for determining the boundaries of congressional and state legislative districts and Board of Equalization districts.

city council The governing body of a city; members are elected at large or by district to four-year terms.

city manager The top administrative officer in most California cities; appointed by the city council.

civil service system A system for hiring and retaining public employees on the basis of their qualifications or merit; replaced the political machine's patronage, or spoils, system; encompasses 98 percent of state workers.

closed primary An election of party nominees in which only registered party members may participate.

collegiality Deferential behavior among justices as a way of building consensus on issues before the court.

Commission on Judicial Appointments A commission to review and make recommendations on the governor's nominees for appellate and supreme courts; consists of the attorney general, the chief justice of the state supreme court, and the senior presiding judge of the courts of appeal.

Commission on Judicial Performance The state board empowered to investigate charges of judicial misconduct or incompetence.

conference committee A committee of senate and assembly members that meets to reconcile different versions of the same bill.

congressional delegation Members of the House of Representatives and Senate representing a particular state.

consolidation The merger of cities, school districts, or special districts; usually requires voter approval.

Constitution of 1849 California's first constitution, which was copied from constitutions of other states and featured a two-house legislature, a supreme court, and an executive branch including a governor, lieutenant governor, controller, attorney general, and superintendent of public instruction, as well as a bill of rights. Only white males were allowed to vote.

Constitution of 1879 California's second constitution, which retained the basic structures of the Constitution of 1849 but added institutions to regulate railroads and public utilities and to ensure fair tax assessments. Chinese individuals were denied the right to vote, own land, or work for the government.

constitutional amendments May be placed on the ballot by a two-thirds vote of the legislature or through the initiative process; must be approved by a simple majority of the voters.

constitutional convention An occasion for extensive revision or reform of the state constitution. A two-thirds vote of the state legislature is required to put a proposal for a convention on the ballot. If voters approve, delegates are elected by district.

contract lobbyist An individual or company that represents the interests of clients before the legislature and other policymaking entities.

contracting for services Smaller cities contract with counties, special districts, other cities, or private companies to provide services they cannot efficiently provide themselves.

controller An independently elected state executive who oversees taxing and spending.

council–manager system A form of government in which an elected council appoints a professional manager to administer daily operations; used by most California cities.

councils of government (COGs) Regional planning organizations with representation for cities and counties.

counties Local governments and administrative agencies of the state, run by elected boards of supervisors; principal responsibilities include welfare, jails, courts, roads, and elections.

county executive The top administrative officer in most California counties; appointed by the board of supervisors.

courts of appeal Three-justice panels that hear appeals from lower courts.

cross-filing An election system that allowed candidates to win the nomination of more than one political party; eliminated in 1959.

demographic groups Interest groups based on race, ethnicity, gender, or age; usually concerned with overcoming discrimination.

direct democracy Progressive reforms giving citizens the power to make and repeal laws (initiative and referendum) and to remove elected officials from office (recall).

direct mail A campaign technique by which candidates communicate selected messages to selected voters by mail.

director of finance The state officer primarily responsible for preparation of the budget; appointed by the governor.

district attorney The chief prosecuting officer elected in each county; represents the people against the accused in criminal cases.

district elections Elections in which candidates are chosen by only one part of the city, county, or state.

economic groups Interest groups with sizable financial stakes in the political process who seek to influence legislators and other public policymakers.

Environmental Protection Agency (EPA) The federal government body charged with carrying out national environmental policy objectives.

executive order The power of the governor to make rules that have the effect of laws; may be overturned by the legislature.

Fair Political Practices Commission (FPPC) Established by the Political Reform Act of 1974, this independent regulatory commission monitors candidates' campaign finance reports and lobbyists.

federalism The distribution of power, resources, and responsibilities among the national, state, and local governments.

fiscalization of land use Cities and counties, when making land use decisions, opt for the alternative that produces the most revenue.

general elections Statewide elections held on the first Tuesday after the first Monday of November in even-numbered years. Voter turnout is higher than in primary elections and highest during presidential elections.

general-law city or county A city or county whose organization and structure of government are derived from state law.

general veto The gubernatorial power to reject an entire bill or budget; overruled only by an absolute two-thirds vote of both houses of the state legislature.

ghost voting When legislators cast electronic votes in place of assembly members who are not at their posts; this practice is against the law.

governor California's highest-ranking executive officeholder; elected every four years.

grants-in-aid Payments from the national government to states to assist in fulfilling public policy objectives.

gut-and-amend The process of removing the original provisions from a bill and inserting new, unrelated content, usually at the last minute.

incorporation The process by which residents of an urbanized area form a city.

independent expenditures Campaign spending by interest groups and political action committees on behalf of candidates.

initiative A Progressive device by which people may put laws and constitutional amendments on the ballot after securing the required number of voters' signatures.

instant runoff voting Voters rank candidates in order of preference. If no candidate wins a majority, the candidate with the fewest votes is eliminated, and those votes are assigned to the voters' second choice—and so on until one candidate attains a majority.

insurance commissioner An elected state executive who regulates the insurance industry; created by a 1988 initiative.

interest group An organized group of individuals sharing common political objectives who actively attempt to influence policymakers.

item veto The power of the governor to delete or reduce the budget within a bill without rejecting the entire bill or budget; an absolute two-thirds vote of both houses of the state legislature is required to override.

judicial activism Making policy through court decisions rather than through the legislative or electoral process.

Judicial Council Chaired by the chief justice of the state supreme court and composed of twenty-one judges and attorneys; makes the rules for court procedures, collects data on the courts' operations and workload, and gives seminars for judges.

legislative analyst An assistant to the legislature who studies the annual budget and proposed programs.

legislative committees Small groups of senators or assembly members who consider and make legislation in specialized areas such as agriculture or education.

legislative counsel Assists the legislature in preparing bills and assessing their impact on existing legislation.

legislative initiatives Propositions placed on the ballot by the legislature rather than by citizen petition.

lieutenant governor The chief executive when the governor is absent from the state or disabled; succeeds the governor in case of death or other departure from office; casts a tiebreaking vote in the senate; is independently elected.

litigation An interest group tactic of challenging a law or policy in the courts to have it overruled, modified, or delayed.

lobbying Interest group efforts to influence political decision makers, often through paid professionals (lobbyists).

local agency formation commission (LAFCO) A county agency set up to oversee the creation and expansion of cities.

logrolling A give-and-take process in which legislators trade support for each other's bills.

mayor The ceremonial leader of a city; usually a position that alternates among council members, but in some large cities the mayor is directly elected and given substantial powers.

nonpartisan elections A Progressive reform that removed party labels from ballots for local and judicial offices.

personal income tax A graduated tax on individual earnings adopted in 1935; the largest source of state revenues.

plea bargaining An agreement between the prosecution and the accused in which the latter pleads guilty to a reduced charge and lesser penalty.

political action committees (PACs) Mechanisms by which interest groups direct campaign contributions to preferred candidates.

political consultants Expert professionals in political campaigning available for hire; most consultants work exclusively for candidates of one of the major political parties.

Political Reform Act of 1974 An initiative requiring officials to disclose conflicts of interest, campaign contributions, and spending; also requires lobbyists to register with the Fair Political Practices Commission.

preprimary endorsement Political parties' designation of preferred candidates in party primary elections, thus strengthening the role of party organizations in selecting candidates; banned by state law until 1990.

president pro tem The legislative leader of the state senate; chairs the Rules Committee; selected by the majority party.

primary elections Elections to choose nominees for public office; held in June of even-numbered years. Voter turnout is typically low.

Progressives Members of an anti-machine reform movement that reshaped the state's political institutions between 1907 and the 1920s.

property tax A tax on land and buildings; until the passage of Proposition 13 in 1978, the primary source of revenues for local governments.

Proposition 1A (2008) A $10 billion bond passed by the voters to begin construction of a high-speed rail system; officially called the Safe, Reliable High-Speed Passenger Train Bond Act for the 21st Century.

Proposition 8 (2008) An initiative that amended the state constitution to restrict marriage to opposite-sex couples.

Proposition 11, Voters FIRST Initiative (2008) An initiative that placed legislative redistricting in the hands of a fourteen-member citizens commission instead of the state legislature.

Proposition 13 (1978) Also known as the Jarvis-Gann initiative; a ballot measure that cut property taxes and significantly reduced revenues for local governments.

Proposition 22, California Defense of Marriage Act (2000) A ballot initiative that declared marriage an act between a man and a woman.

Proposition 22, Local Taxpayers, Public Safety, and Transportation Act (2010) An initiative that keeps the state government from taking local government funds.

Proposition 25, Majority Vote for the Legislature to Pass the Budget Act (2010) An initiative that lowered the votes required for the legislature to pass a budget from two-thirds to a simple majority.

Proposition 28, California Change Term Limits Initiative (2012) An initiative which allows state legislators to serve for no more than twelve years in either house of the legislature, with no restrictions on how they divide their time.

Proposition 30 (2012) Governor Brown's initiative to increase sales taxes for five years and income taxes for affluent Californians for seven years.

Proposition 36 (2012) An initiative that made it easier for nonviolent "three strikes" convicts to petition for reduced sentences.

Proposition 98 (1988) An initiative awarding public education a fixed percentage of the state budget.

Proposition 140 (1990) An initiative limiting assembly members to three 2-year terms and senators and statewide elected officials to two 4-year terms and cutting the legislature's budget.

Proposition 187 (1994) An initiative reducing government benefits for illegal immigrants; parts of Proposition 187 were declared unconstitutional by federal courts in 1995.

Proposition 209 (1996) An initiative that eliminated affirmative action in California.

Proposition 227 (1998) An initiative limiting bilingual education to no more than one year.

public defender A county officer representing defendants who cannot afford an attorney; appointed by the county board of supervisors.

public interest groups Organizations that purport to represent the general good rather than private interests.

realignment The transfer of some state-provided services to counties, most recently observed with the movement of state prisoners to county jails.

reapportionment The adjustment of legislative district boundaries to keep all districts equal in population; done every ten years after the national census; done by a citizens commission beginning in 2011.

recall A Progressive reform allowing voters to remove elected officials by petition and majority vote.

redistricting Another term for reapportionment, the adjustment of legislative districts by population every ten years.

referendum A Progressive reform requiring the legislature to place certain measures before the voters, who may also repeal legislation by petitioning for a referendum.

register to vote Citizens who are over eighteen years of age and who are not incarcerated or in a mental institution are eligible to sign up to vote by completion of a registration form. Nearly 30 percent of those eligible to register in California do not do so and thus cannot participate in elections.

Reynolds v. Sims A 1964 U.S. Supreme Court decision that ordered redistricting of the upper houses of all state legislatures by population instead of land area.

Rules Committee *See Senate Rules Committee.*

runoff election When no candidate receives more than 50 percent of the vote in a nonpartisan primary for trial court judge or local office, the top two candidates face each other in a runoff.

sales tax A statewide tax on most goods and products; adopted in 1933; local governments receive a portion of this tax.

school districts Local governments created by states to provide elementary and secondary education; governed by elected school boards.

secretary of state An elected state executive who keeps election records and supervises elections.

Senate Rules Committee A five-member committee consisting of the senate president pro tem and two other members from each party in the senate; assigns chairs and committee appointments; functions as the gatekeeper of most senate legislation.

Silicon Valley The top area for high-tech industries; located between San Jose and San Francisco.

single-issue groups Organized groups with narrow policy objectives; not oriented toward compromise.

Southern Pacific Railroad A railroad company founded in 1861; developed a political machine that dominated California state politics through the turn of the century.

Speaker of the assembly The legislative leader of the assembly; selected by the majority party; controls committee appointments and the legislative process.

special districts Local government agencies providing a single service, such as fire protection or sewage disposal.

special session A legislative session called by the governor; limited to discussion of topics specified by the governor.

state auditor An assistant to the legislature who analyzes ongoing programs.

superintendent of public instruction The elected state executive in charge of public education.

superior courts Lower courts in which criminal and civil cases are first tried.

supreme court California's highest judicial body; hears appeals from lower courts.

term limits Limits on the number of terms that officeholders may serve; elected executive branch officers and state senators are limited to two 4-year terms, and assembly members are limited to three 2-year terms. Some local elected officials are limited to two or three 4-year terms.

termed out An elected official must leave office when he or she has completed all the terms of office allowed under California's term limits law.

third parties Minor political parties that capture a small percentages of the vote in the general election but are viewed as important protest vehicles.

"three strikes" A 1994 law and initiative requiring sentences of twenty-five years to life for anyone convicted of three felonies.

top-two primary Voters in primary elections may cast their ballots for any listed candidate for an office irrespective of the voters' party affiliation; the top two vote winners proceed to a runoff in the general election; instituted by a 2010 ballot measure; first in effect in 2012.

treasurer The elected state executive responsible for managing state funds between collection and spending.

user taxes Taxes on select commodities or services "used" by those who benefit directly from them; examples include gasoline taxes and cigarette taxes.

veto See *general veto* and *item veto*.

vote by mail Voters who prefer not to vote at their polling places or who are unable to vote on Election Day may apply to their county registrar of voters for an absentee ballot and vote by mail or register as permanent absentee voters; over half of those who vote in California elections vote by mail.

voter turnout The proportion of eligible and/or registered voters who actually participate in an election. When turnout is high, the electorate is usually more diverse and liberal; when it is low, the electorate is usually older, more affluent, and more conservative.

Workingmen's Party Denis Kearney's antirailroad, anti-Chinese organization; instrumental in rewriting California's constitution in 1879.

Index